Teddy Bear Storytimes

Ready-to-Go Flannel and Magnetic Storyboard Programs That Captivate Children

LaDonna Yousha

Neal-Schuman Publishers, Inc.

New York   London

Published by Neal-Schuman Publishers, Inc.
100 William St., Suite 2004
New York, NY 10038

Copyright © 2009 Neal-Schuman Publishers, Inc.

Printed and bound in the United States of America.

The paper used in this publication meets the minimum requirements of American National Standard for Information Sciences-Permanence of Paper for Printed Library Materials, ANSI Z39.48-1992.

Library of Congress Cataloging-in-Publication Data

Yousha, LaDonna, 1968-
    Teddy Bear storytimes : ready-to-go flannel and magnetic storyboard programs that captivate children / LaDonna Yousha.
        p. cm.
    Includes indexes.
    ISBN 978-1-55570-677-7 (alk. paper)
    1. Storytelling—United States. 2. Children's libraries—Activity programs—United States. 3. Flannel boards. 4. Children's stories, American. I. Title.

Z718.3.Y68 2009
027.62'51—dc22

                                                                        2009003626

Contents

List of Figures

List of Patterns

Acknowledgments

Thanks to my real family of bears: Father Bear Eric, Grandma Bear Pauline, and my three little bears, Evelyn, Noah, and Jacob.

Thank you to my editor, RoseMary Honnold, who put it all together.

Thank you to the children and staff at the Queens Borough Public Library, the Great Neck Library, and the Wee Friends School who listened to every story and gave me a reason to write this book.

Special thanks go to Dave and Tam Morhaim for all their work on the illustrations. Thank you!

Preface

I love telling stories; I also love helping parents, other librarians, and anyone who works with young children become adept and comfortable in the role of storyteller.

I wrote *Teddy Bear Storytimes: Ready-to-Go Flannel and Magnetic Storyboard Programs That Captivate Children* with busy educators and other storytellers in mind. Patterns on the accompanying CD-ROM, ready-made book lists for finding other stories with similar themes, and clear instructions on creating storyboards make this an excellent resource for storytellers who are pressed for time. Both novice and experienced storytellers will find among these pages a wealth of storytime ideas easily adapted to any program setting.

The flannel or magnetic board is a wonderful way to share stories with young children. Children are captivated by the stories and by the figures that seem to dance in front of their eyes. They love the "magic" way the characters stick on the board. My storytime children started calling it the "magic" board, and that's what it has been called in my library ever since. I feature an interactive "magic" board story in all of my storyhours because the response is always enthusiastic. Finding the perfect story that works well for the "magic" board week after week has not always been so easy, though. Nor is it always a given that I have enough time to make the figures for the board.

I started making up my own stories for the board. I create stories that children can relate to based on themes that interest them. In addition, the stories always include an element of movement.

The character of Teddy Bear consistently brings both comfort and familiarity to storytime. Children look forward to seeing and hearing about Teddy Bear and his family. In fact, I had to stop putting Teddy Bear on the board before storytime because the children would chant, "Teddy Bear, Teddy Bear." Then, I would have to start with the story on the "magic" board before continuing with storytime. Children love to hear stories involving a beloved character that is well known to them. Just look at the popularity of such characters as Curious George, Arthur, Clifford, Spot, Maisy, and Olivia, to name just a few. The children look forward to the next Teddy Bear adventure.

Why Use Flannel or Magnetic Boards?

Children find the flannel or magnetic board "magical." They are filled with wonder as the characters come alive right in front of them. "Magic" board stories also provide opportunities for the audience to participate in the story. Children can join in with the actions and dialogue of the characters. Children use their imaginations as they travel with the characters into outer space, to the circus, and on many more adventures.

The storyteller can interact more freely with the audience as well. The storyteller is free to move around, demonstrate actions, and have more eye contact with the audience. It is essentially storytelling with props. "Magic" board stories are perfect for the beginner storyteller, because the characters and figures help with the sequence of the story.

Making a flannel board is an easy and inexpensive project. All you need is some heavy cardboard, felt to cover it, glue, and tape. I use a trifold project display board (most often used for science projects). The trifold design allows for safe and clean transport, as you can fold it over to close.

The boards are usually 48 inches wide by 36 inches high. I cut off 12 inches from the top to make it more portable. Have enough black felt to cover the entire height of the board plus a few inches overlap, and glue it to the board. (Felt is sold in most craft stores in a variety of sizes, including by the yard.) Reinforce with tape on the back of the board. This makes a 48-by-24-inch flannel board that allows better viewing and that is able to accommodate a larger audience. The patterns in this book work best on a flannel board of at least 36 inches wide and 24 inches high.

How to Use This Book

The chapters in this book are organized by themes, so first choose a theme that's right for the calendar, the audience, and your mood. Within each theme is a complete storytime experience, including a list of the characters and figures needed as well as directions on how to tell the story and on how to move the figures. Accompanying photographs illustrate where to place the figures (see the accompanying CD-ROM for color versions). Each story is followed by a list of books to read aloud and playful activities to expand on the chapter's theme.

The sections within each chapter are as follows:

- Characters and Story Pieces Needed
- Directions for the Story
- The Story
- Books to Read Aloud
- Ideas for Playful Activities

Characters and Story Pieces Needed

The characters are Teddy Bear and his family. Teddy Bear is a loving, safe, and comfortable character that children love. They enjoy the continuing adventures of Teddy Bear every time they attend storytime. This section lists which bear characters and figures you will need. The patterns for all of these pieces are both printed in the back of the book, along with some ideas on how to embellish and make them your own, and included on the accompanying CD-ROM.

Because the bears are supposed to be warm and cuddly, felt is the perfect fabric to use. You can buy felt at your local craft store. It is usually sold in 9-by-12-inch pieces or by the yard, which can save you some money. Copy or print the patterns, and cut them out. Trace the patterns onto felt with a black fine tip permanent marker. Use the black fine tip marker to draw the faces as well. Color the patterns, laminate them, and place Velcro on their backs (see also the Appendix for optional embellishments).

If you are using a magnetic board, I still recommend using felt for the bear characters. You can find magnetic tape at your local craft store. You can easily apply it to the backs of the figures, and it will stick to any magnetic board. For the other figures, you can copy/print and cut out the patterns, color them, and apply magnetic tape.

Directions for the Story

This section provides directions on how to arrange the story on the board. It is much easier to have the figures in order before starting the story. It will also help you remember the sequence of the story. For those stories ("Teddy Bear's Garden" and "Teddy Bear Is a Magician") for which other pieces are placed on top or behind other pieces, add Velcro to make the composite adhere more firmly to the board. For example, for the story "Teddy Bear's Garden," glue a piece of Velcro or use self-adhesive Velcro (hook side) dots and stick them to the flower in two spots. When you hide the bugs behind the leaf or petal, they will not fall off when you take the bug away.

The Story

The story immediately follows the directions. Stories included in this book are all very easy to remember and tell. Many are repetitive, so you just have to memorize the refrain. I strongly recommend that you do not read from the book when telling the story. You can memorize the story or use cue cards so that you can interact more with your audience and enjoy the story to a greater extent. Encourage the children to participate by having them join in at the refrain, demonstrate actions that go along with the story, and interact with the characters.

Books to Read Aloud

I then recommend several books with the same theme as the chapters to read aloud. I include newer titles as well as classics. Choose two or three books from the list to complete your storytime. Most of the books are in print, and all should be readily available from your school or public library.

Ideas for Playful Activities

This section lists fun stretches and physical activities that expand on the theme. Each chapter includes a song, fingerplay, or game to play. The activities give ample opportunity for children to act out songs, use their imaginations, and spark their creativity. This, along with the interactive nature of the "magic" board stories, allows children to become more involved in storytime.

The only imperative for storytellers is to enjoy the story, enjoy the children, and radiate enthusiasm for reading. I hope the tools in this book and on the accompanying CD-ROM and my good friends the Bear Family will help make your storytimes both easier and more enjoyable.

1
Teddy Bear Plays Baseball:
Learning to Be a Good Sport

"Teddy Bear Plays Baseball" is a story all children can relate to. Teddy Bear doesn't like baseball, because he doesn't think he is any good at it. Children will love that Teddy Bear is like them and has to keep trying to succeed. In the end, he learns the importance of good sportsmanship and to just have fun.

Characters and Story Pieces Needed

Father Bear	Teddy Bear	Clouds (2)
Mother Bear	Bat	Chicken
Billy Bear	Baseball	Cow
Claire Bear	Moon	Pig

Directions for the Story

Place Teddy Bear on the board, with the clouds in the upper right corner of the board. When the story mentions Teddy Bear's family members, put them on the board as well. When they play ball, have the characters hold the bat and place the ball as if they hit it. Have the ball touch the clouds or the moon as the story dictates.

Hold up the appropriate number of fingers when the characters say, "Strike one! Strike two! Strike three!" For more movement, have the children pretend to hold a bat and concentrate on hitting the pretend ball.

FIGURE 1.1. Teddy Bear Plays Baseball

The Story

TEDDY BEAR PLAYS BASEBALL

This is Teddy Bear, and he has waited all year for baseball season! Teddy Bear and his big brother love baseball. So do their sister Claire Bear, Mother Bear, and Father Bear. They watch it on TV and watch it live at the stadium, but most of all they love to play baseball. So one day they were at the park playing, and big brother Billy Bear was up first. The ball was pitched and "Pow!" Billy Bear hit the ball and it flew toward the sky. It seemed to touch the clouds.

"Wow!" said Teddy Bear. Now it was Teddy Bear's turn. He held the bat, he watched the ball, but . . .

"Strike one!"

"Strike two!"

"Strike three!"

"You're out!" they shouted.

"Oh!" cried Teddy Bear. "I don't like baseball anymore! I'm not any good, and I'm not playing anymore!"

But the next day...

The Bear Family went to the stadium to watch a baseball game. The game was so exciting. "Go, Team, Go!" They roared. "Go, Team, Go!" So, when they got home, they wanted to play. Claire Bear was up first. "Pow!" She hit the ball and it went up to the sky. It seemed to touch the moon! Teddy Bear was next. He held the bat, he watched the ball, but...

"Strike one!"

"Strike two!"

"Strike three!"

"You're out!" they shouted.

"Oh, no!" cried Teddy Bear. "I don't like baseball anymore!"

But, the next day after school, he saw his friends playing in the ball field. They were having so much fun.

"Come play!" they called to Teddy Bear. He said he would just watch. Peggy Pig was up first. She held the bat, she watched the ball, but ...

"Strike one!"

"Strike two!"

"Strike three!"

"You're out!" they shouted, but Peggy did not get mad.

"Go, Team, Go!" she said. Charlie Chicken was up next, and "Thud!" the ball rolled down center field. Charlie made it to first base.

"Go, Team, Go!" everyone shouted. Cameron Cow saw Teddy Bear watching.

"Come and play," he called.

"I'm not that good," answered Teddy Bear.

"That's okay," said Cameron Cow, "We're just having fun."

"Okay," said Teddy Bear, and he took the bat. He held the bat, he watched the ball, but...

"Strike one!"

"Strike two!"

"It's okay," Teddy said to himself. "I'm still having fun." He closed his eyes and swung the bat. "Pow!" He heard the ball hit the bat, and it flew up into the air—not as high as the clouds, not as high as the moon, but it did go pretty high. "Yeah!" everyone shouted. "Go, Team, Go!"

"I love baseball!" yelled Teddy Bear.

Books About Sports to Read Aloud

Alborough, Jez. 2005. *Hit the Ball Duck*. La Jolla, CA: Kane/Miller.

Kraus, Robert. 2000. *Mort the Sport*. Illustrated by John Himelman. New York: Orchard Books.

London, Jonathon. 2007. *Froggy Plays T-Ball*. Illustrated by Frank Remkiewicz. New York: Viking.

Paxton, Tom. 1999. *Jungle Baseball Game*. Illustrated by Karen Lee Schmidt. New York: Morrow Junior Books.

Ideas for Playful Activities

Sing a Song

Sing "Take Me Out to the Ballgame." The song is available on Bob McGrath's CD *If You're Happy and You Know It: Sing Along with Bob*, Vol. 1 (Bob's Kids Music, 2000).

Get Active

Play sport charades. One child acts out playing a sport (baseball, soccer, football, swimming, ice-skating, etc.), while the other children guess what the sport is. Offer choices by writing names of sports on paper or, for pre-readers, showing them clip art pictures from the Internet.

2

The Bear Family Goes to the Circus:

A Hide-n-Seek Story

The circus is a fun theme for children. Children will enjoy looking for the Bear Family in an interactive hide-n-seek story. The activities included involve a lot of audience participation—from juggling scarves to balancing on a tightrope!

Characters and Story Pieces Needed

Father Bear	Mailbox	Dirt
Mother Bear	Couch	Bed
Billy Bear	Table	Blanket
Claire Bear	Flowers	Car
Teddy Bear		

Directions for the Story

Set up the board beforehand with the garden scene on the left side with the mailbox. Place the table, couch, and bed on the right. Hide the appropriate teddy bear behind the couch, table, etc., according to the story, letting only a tiny piece of the teddy bears stick out. Place the car with Father Bear on the board at the appropriate time. The children will enjoy repeating the refrain.

FIGURE 2.1. The Bear Family Goes to the Circus

The Story

THE BEAR FAMILY GOES TO THE CIRCUS

One day, Mother Bear went to the mailbox and opened the mail. Five tickets to the circus! "Hurray!" she yelled. She went into the house. "Where is everybody?" she asked. She had to find her family. Mother Bear called to Billy Bear.

> Billy Bear, Billy Bear
> Where is he?
> Billy Bear, Billy Bear
> Where can he be?

There he is! He is behind the couch playing hide and seek.

> Hurry, hurry.
> Don't be late.
> The circus is in town.
> It will be great!

Teddy Bear, Teddy Bear
Where is he?
Teddy Bear, Teddy Bear
Where can he be?

Teddy Bear is under the covers playing peek-a-boo!

Hurry, hurry.
Don't be late.
The circus is in town.
It will be great!

Where is Claire Bear? There she is, playing in the garden! Everybody looks for Father Bear. Not under the table. Not behind the couch. Not in the garden.

Father Bear, Father Bear
Where is he?
Father Bear, Father Bear
Where can he be?

"Here I am," said Father Bear. He's already in the car! [*Place the car with Father Bear on the board.*] Now the Bear Family can go to the circus!

Books About the Circus to Read Aloud

Ehlert, Lois. 1992. *Circus*. New York: HarperCollins.
Falconer, Ian. 2001. *Olivia Saves the Circus*. New York: Atheneum.
Paxton, Tom. 1997. *Engelbert Joins the Circus*. Illustrated by Roberta Wilson. New York: William Morrow.
Stadler, John. 2007. *Big and Little*. New York: Robin Carey Books.
Ziefert, Harriet. 2005. *Circus Parade*. Pictures by Tanya Roitman. Maplewood, NJ: Blue Apple Books.

Ideas for Playful Activities

Get Active

Have the children put on their own circus. Pretend they are lions and go through a hula hoop. Act like clowns and juggle scarves or be tightrope walkers and balance on top of a jump rope on the floor. Pretend to be dancing elephants by standing on their tippy toes and turning around or linking arms and walking in an elephant parade.

Act out circus scenes with Georgiana Stewart's CD *Do It Yourself Kids Circus* (Kimbo Educational, 1980).

Perform Magic

Do an easy magic trick in which a circus picture magically colors itself! You can buy one for about $6.50 from Clown Antics, Inc. Search their Web site (www.clownantics.com) for "Circus Picture Frame" or find it under "Magic Tricks" in the category "General Magic and Illusions." (You can also call them at 734-454-6625.)

Clown Antics also sells great magic coloring books with a clown theme. Look in the category "Coloring Books and Drawing Magic." Try the *Clown Coloring Book* by Royal Magic ($7.50).

3

Who Lives in the Garden?
A Riddle Story

There are many wonderful books and activities with a garden theme. The story in this chapter is also a riddle game. Children learn about garden bugs in a fun way with this story. In the activity section, children will pretend to grow from tiny seeds into a beautiful garden!

Characters and Story Pieces Needed

Teddy Bear	Dirt	Ladybug
Watering can	Grass	Worm
Hat	Bee	Spider
Flowers	Butterfly	

Directions for the Story

Velcro the flowers to the board so they will better hide the bugs. Hide all the bugs (except the butterfly) before you start. Place the bee under a flower. Place the ladybug under a flower leaf. Place the worm under the dirt, and hide the spider between the grass and dirt. Have the children guess what is hiding before you take the pieces off. Flutter the butterfly through the air and around the children. The children will enjoy making the sounds and motions of the bugs.

FIGURE 3.1. Who Lives in the Garden?

The Story

WHO LIVES IN THE GARDEN?

Teddy Bear is carrying a watering can. Where is he going? He puts on his hat and walks into the garden. There's something buzzing around the flowers, hiding in the petals. It is collecting pollen and carrying it home to its hive. What could it be? A bee! [*Lift up the flower petal.*] Help the bee buzz away ("Buzz, Buzz, Buzz").

There is something hiding under the leaf. It helps Teddy Bear in the garden by eating aphids, which would destroy his flowers. It is beautiful in red with black polka dots. What could it be? A ladybug! [*Lift up the leaf.*] Help the ladybug fly away. [*Make tiny wings with your hands.*]

What is hiding in the dirt? Something is squirming and wiggling. It is helping Teddy Bear by making the soil rich and healthy so plants and flowers can grow. A worm! [*Lift up the patch of dirt.*] Help the worm wiggle away. [*Wiggle your pointer finger away behind your back.*]

There is something fluttering by. It flutters from flower to flower, sipping nectar along its way. It is colorful and beautiful. A butterfly! [*Place the butterfly on the board.*] Help the butterfly flutter away. [*Make wings with your hands and fly away.*]

Teddy Bear spies something creeping in the grass. It hangs from silken thread and dangles among the blades. A spider! Help the spider creep away. [*Make a spider with your hands and creep away.*]

Books About Gardens to Read Aloud

Ayres, Katherine. 2007. *Up, Down and Around*. Illustrated by Nadine Bernard Westcott. Cambridge, MA: Candlewick Press.

Bruce, Lisa. 2002. *Fran's Flower*. Illustrated by Rosalind Beardshaw. New York: HarperCollins.

Bunting, Eve. 1999. *Flower Garden*. Illustrated by Kathryn Hewitt. San Diego: Harcourt Brace.

Ehlert, Lois. 1988. *Planting a Rainbow*. San Diego: Harcourt Brace Jovanovich.

Fleming, Candace. 2007. *Tippy-Tippy-Tippy-Hide*. Illustrated by G. Brian Karas. New York: Atheneum Books for Young Readers.

George Lindsay Barrett. 2006. *In the Garden: Who's Been Here?* New York: Greenwillow Books.

Wellington, Monica. 2005. *Zinnia's Flower Garden*. New York: Dutton Children's Books.

Ideas for Playful Activities

Sing a Song

Sing "I'm a Little Seed" from Carole Peterson's CD *Tiny Tunes* (Carole Peterson, 2005).

Have fun singing about various garden creatures like the "eensy weensy spider" and the caterpillar in "Arabella Miller," both from Sharon, Lois, and Bram's CD *Mainly Mother Goose* (Casablanca Kids, 2005).

Get Active

Have the children pretend they are tiny seeds in the ground, and then have them grow tall. Pretend the flowers are swaying in the breeze, getting rained on or leaning toward the sun. Ask them what type of flower they are.

4

A Pirate Adventure for Teddy Bear:
Learning to Be a Good Friend

Pirates are a favorite theme of young children. Children can sing, dance, and talk like pirates. In this chapter, Teddy Bear learns how to be a good friend. He realizes that when you have a group of friends sometimes you have to take turns choosing what game to play. This chapter also gives children a chance to read a map as they locate treasure!

Characters and Story Pieces Needed

Teddy Bear	Pig	Pirate map
Cow	Shovel	Tree
Chicken	Dirt	

Directions for the Story

Place all of the figures on the board before you start. Put Teddy Bear and all his friends on the right side of the board next to the dirt, with the map hidden under it. Place the tree on the far left. When Teddy Bear finds the map, pull it out and show it to the children. Move Teddy Bear under the tree with his shovel. End the story with all the characters back on the board.

FIGURE 4.1. A Pirate Adventure for Teddy Bear

The Story

A PIRATE ADVENTURE FOR TEDDY BEAR

Teddy Bear loves everything to do with pirates. Most of all he loves to play pirates with his friends. But his friends want to play something else today.

"Let's play ball," said Cameron Cow.

"Let's play tag," said Charlie Chicken.

"Let's play superheroes," said Peggy Pig.

"No," said Teddy Bear, "I don't want to play any of those games. I want to play pirates. So I'll play by myself!"

"Okay," said his friends sadly, and they ran off to play together.

Teddy Bear sang pirate songs. "Yo, ho, ho, it's a pirate's life for me!" He danced pirate dances. He even tried to sound like a pirate—"Aaarrgh!"—but it was not the same without his friends. Teddy Bear was lonely with no one to play pirates with.

Teddy Bear thought his friends would be upset with him, so instead of joining them he took his shovel and dug in the dirt for a while. All of a sudden he felt something. It looked like a map. It was a pirate map! He looked at the map and found an X mark. Do you see the X on the map?

Teddy Bear saw that the X was under a tree. Do you see the tree? Teddy Bear started digging. He wondered if there would be jewels like diamonds, sapphires, and emeralds, or maybe there would be gold! He thought of all the treasure he would dig up. He would be rich! He wished his friends were with him. All of a sudden he heard a voice.

"Can I dig with you?" asked Cameron Cow.

"Sure," said Teddy Bear. He was so happy that someone wanted to play with him. They dug, dug, and dug. Still they didn't find any treasure.

"I'm sorry we didn't find a treasure," said Cameron Cow.

"That's okay," said Teddy Bear. "I found something better than treasure. I found a friend to play with!" Teddy Bear asked Cameron Cow if he wanted to play ball now. And after that they would play tag with Charlie Chicken and superheroes with Peggy Pig so everyone would get a turn to choose a game.

Books About Pirates to Read Aloud

Harris, Peter. 2006. *The Night Pirates.* Illustrated by Deborah Allwright. New York: Scholastic Press.

Krosoczka, Jarrett. 2003. *Bubble Bath Pirates!* New York: Viking.

Long, Melinda. 2003. *How I Became a Pirate.* Illustrated by David Shannon. Orlando: Harcourt.

Sturges, Philemon. 2005. *This Little Pirate.* Illustrated by Amy Walrod. New York: Dutton Children's Books.

Tucker, Kathy. 1994. *Do Pirates Take Baths?* Illustrated by Nadine Westcott. Morton Grove, IL: A. Whitman.

Ideas for Playful Activities

Sing a Song

Sing this song about a "Pirate Adventure" (to the tune of "Here We Go Round the Mulberry Bush"):

This is the way the pirates steer their ship, steer their ship, steer their ship.
This is way the pirates steer the ship so they can find some treasure.

This is the way the pirates look at the map, look at the map, look at the map.
This is the way the pirates look at the map so they can find some treasure.

This is the way the pirates dig for gold, dig for gold, dig for gold.
This is the way the pirates dig for gold so they can find some treasure.

This is the way the pirates do a dance, do a dance, do a dance.

This is the way the pirates do a dance because they found some treasure.

Read a Pirate Map

Children love to pretend they are pirates. Have them go on a treasure hunt around the room. Draw up a simple map of the room with a big X where they can find the treasure. I usually have two children at a time search for the treasure, which is hidden underneath a chair or behind a book. As an alternative, have the children point to where they think it is hidden, and you can pretend to dig up the treasure. Fill a box with stickers or small prizes for the treasure.

5
Wiggle with the Bear Family:
We All Have the Wiggles

Children need to wiggle a little during storytime. This story gives them an opportunity to wiggle, giggle, jiggle, and tickle! This story can also be told as a fingerplay. Have the children hold up five fingers, with the pinkie as Teddy Bear. It is a great transition to storytime when Teddy Bear says, "Let's read a book." Have a book ready to read.

Characters and Story Pieces Needed

Father Bear   Claire Bear

Mother Bear   Teddy Bear

Billy Bear   Book

Directions for the Story

This is a simple story to tell. It is a good transition to quiet the wiggles before storytime. Place the Bear Family on the board. As you speak of the characters, point to them and do the appropriate action. Have fun with the voices and actions in this story, like using a deep voice for Father Bear. Use a tickling motion with your hands for Mother Bear, and so forth. Encourage the children wiggle, tickle, giggle, and jiggle along with you. Have Teddy Bear hold the book at the end of the story.

FIGURE 5.1. Wiggle with the Bear Family

The Story

WIGGLE WITH THE BEAR FAMILY

The Bear Family loves to wiggle!

Father Bear wiggles like this, "wiggle, wiggle, wiggle!" [*Use a deep voice for Father Bear.*]

Mother Bear wiggles with a tickle. Wiggle, wiggle, tickle! [*Tickle with your fingers.*]

Claire Bear wiggles with a giggle. Wiggle, wiggle, giggle! [*Giggle with a high voice.*]

Billy Bear wiggles with a jiggle. Wiggle, wiggle, jiggle! [*Shake your fingers.*]

Teddy Bear wonders why they can't stop the wiggles. . . . "No more wiggles!" he yells. [*Hold up your hand in a stop motion.*]

Still, Father Bear goes wiggle, wiggle, wiggle!

Mother Bear goes wiggle, wiggle, tickle!

Claire Bear goes wiggle, wiggle, giggle!

Billy Bear goes wiggle, wiggle, jiggle!
But Teddy Bear knows how to stop the wiggles. . . . "Let's read a book!" says
Teddy Bear.

Father Bear stops wiggling.
Mother Bear stops tickling.
Claire Bear stops giggling.
Billy Bear stops jiggling.
And Teddy Bear reads a book!

Silly Books to Read Aloud

Cronin, Doreen. 2005. *Wiggle*. Illustrated by Scott Menchin. New York:
 Atheneum Books for Young Readers.
Hills, Tad. 2000. *Knock, Knock! Who's There?* New York: Simon and Schuster
 Children's Publishing.
Lorig, Steffanie and Richard Lorig. 2008. *Such a Silly Baby!* Illustrated by
 Amanda Shepherd. San Francisco: Chronicle Books.
McGee, Marni. 2008. *Silly Goose*. Wiltshire, England: Good Books.
Williams, Mo. 2004. *The Pigeon Finds a Hot Dog!* New York: Hyperion Books
 for Children.
Wood, Audrey. 1992. *Silly Sally*. San Diego: Harcourt Brace Jovanovich.

Ideas for Playful Activities

Sing a Song

Sing and act out the song "Shake Your Sillies Out" by Raffi on the CD
Singable Songs Collection (Rounder, 1997).

Sing and dance to the "Silly Dance Contest," sung by Jim Gill on the CD
Jim Gill Sings the Sneezing Song and Other Contagious Songs (Jim Gill Music,
1993).

Tell a Joke

Tell knock, knock jokes. Have the children tell their favorite jokes.

6

The Bear Family Goes on Vacation:

A Mystery

The story in this chapter will have children guessing where the Bear Family is going for vacation. Children love mysteries and will love trying to figure out the clues. The activities included will have the children up and moving.

Characters and Story Pieces Needed

Father Bear	Teddy Bear	Boat
Mother Bear	Shovel	Sand castle
Billy Bear	Sun	Book
Claire Bear	Ocean	

Directions for the Story

Place Teddy Bear on the board with his family around him. Add pieces as the clues are revealed. Have the children guess where the Bear Family is going. The children will be very excited to guess and will probably know the answer before the end of the story. Tell them they have to wait until the end of the story to see if they are right.

FIGURE 6.1. The Bear Family Goes on Vacation

The Story

THE BEAR FAMILY GOES ON VACATION

The Bear Family is going on vacation for a whole week. That is seven days! The Bear Family is so excited. Teddy Bear wonders where they will go. He thinks about all the places they might visit. The mountains, where there is snow? The desert, where it is so hot? The rain forest, where it rains a lot?

Father Bear tells Teddy Bear he can bring his shovel. [*Put the shovel on the board.*] Teddy thinks they must be going to the mountains where there is snow.

Father Bear tells Teddy Bear that it will be hot and the sun will always be shining where they will be going. [*Put the sun on the board.*] Teddy Bear thinks they will be going to the desert.

But then Father Bear tells him that there will be lots of water. "It can't be the desert," thinks Teddy Bear. "A desert is very dry."

Teddy Bear thinks they are going to the rain forest.

Mother Bear says she can't wait to go for a swim in the water. [*Put the ocean on the board.*]

Claire Bear says she wants to go for a boat ride. [*Put the boat on the board.*]

Billy Bear says he wants to build a sand castle. [*Put the sand castle on the board.*]

Father Bear says he wants to sit in the sun and read a book. [*Put the book on the board.*]

Teddy Bear knows they aren't going to the mountains, desert, or the rain forest. "I know where we are going!" says Teddy Bear.

Do you know where the Bear Family is going?

The Bear Family is going to the beach!

Books About the Beach to Read Aloud

Ashman, Linda. 2005. *To the Beach!* Illustrated by Nadine Bernard Westcott. New York: Harcourt.

Hill, Eric. 1985. *Spot Goes to the Beach*. New York: Putnam.

Hubbell, Patricia. 2001. *Sea, Sand, and Me!* Illustrated by Lisa Campbell Ernst. New York: HarperCollins.

Huneck, Stephen. 2000. *Sally Goes to the Beach*. New York: Abrams.

Lakin, Patricia. 2004. *Beach Day!* Illustrated by Scott Nash. New York: Dial Books for Young Readers.

Roosa, Karen. 2001. *Beach Day*. Illustrated by Maggie Smith. New York: Clarion Books.

Ideas for Playful Activities

Sing a Song

Sing "Mr. Sun" by Raffi on the CD *Singable Songs for the Very Young* (Rounder, 1996).

Get Active

Roll beach balls to each other.

Act Out a Rhyme

Teddy Bear, Teddy Bear,
Swim the back float.
Teddy Bear, Teddy Bear,
Row, row in a boat.
Teddy Bear, Teddy Bear,
Sit in the sun.
Teddy Bear, Teddy Bear,
The day is done.
Teddy Bear, Teddy Bear,
The beach was fun.

7

Teddy Bear's Noisy House:
Let's Make Some Noise!

This story is based on an old Jewish tale. I have heard it told by a great many storytellers. I based this chapter on a version by Mary Garrett (www.story tellermary.com) that I found on Jackie Baldwin's site Story-Lovers.com (http://story-lovers.com/listsnoisyhousestories.html). There are also some great picture book versions that the children might enjoy. Try Margot Zemach's *It Could Always Be Worse* (Farrar, Straus, and Giroux, 1990) or Ann McGovern's *Too Much Noise* (Sandpiper, 1992).

I tell the children this story happened when Teddy Bear was just a baby. All he did was cry! The story is full of repetition, so it is easy to remember and tell. There is also ample opportunity for participation. The children will love making all the sounds of the noisy house. Here is their chance to make noise in the library or classroom.

Characters and Story Pieces Needed

Father Bear	Claire Bear	Drum
Mother Bear	Teddy Bear	Cow
Grandma Bear	Pot	Pig
Billy Bear	Spoon	Chicken

Directions for the Story

Add the characters as they are introduced in the story. Add the story pieces, and make the sound effects. Encourage the children to act out the actions as well. Have them stir soup, sing, bang the drums, cry, etc., with the characters.

FIGURE 7.1. Teddy Bear's Noisy House

Place Grandma Bear in the upper left corner of the board. Father Bear can "climb" up to see her. This is a fun story to exaggerate all the movements!

The Story

TEDDY BEAR'S NOISY HOUSE

Once upon a time, there was a family. There was Mother Bear, Father Bear, Claire Bear, Billy Bear, and baby Teddy Bear.

Mother Bear stirs the chicken soup, "Swosh, Swosh, Swosh." Claire Bear sings, "La, La, La."

Billy Bear plays the drums, "Boom, Boom, Boom."

Teddy Bear cries, "Wah, Wah, Wah."

One day Father Bear came home and heard Mother Bear stirring the soup, "Swosh, Swosh, Swosh." Claire Bear was singing, "La, La, La." Billy Bear was playing the drums, "Boom, Boom, Boom." Teddy Bear was crying, "Wah, Wah, Wah." Father Bear cries out, "I love my family, but it's too noisy!"

Father Bear decided to go ask wise old Grandma Bear for advice. So he walks up the hill to see her. Father Bear says, "I love my family, but they are too noisy. What can I do?" The wise old woman tells Father Bear to bring the cow into the house.

"The cow?" asks Father Bear.

"Yes," says wise old Grandma Bear, "bring the cow into the house." So Father Bear takes the cow from the barn and brings it into the house.

The next day he comes home and hears Mother Bear stirring the soup, "Swosh, Swosh, Swosh."

Claire Bear is singing, "La, La, La."

Billy Bear is playing the drums, "Boom, Boom, Boom."

Teddy Bear is crying, "Wah, Wah, Wah."

And the cow is mooing, "Moo, Moo, Moo."

"It's too noisy!" cries Father Bear. He climbs the hill again. Wise old Grandma Bear tells him to bring the pig into the house.

"The pig?" asks Father Bear.

"Yes, the pig," says the wise Grandma Bear. So Father Bear brings the pig into the house.

The next day Father Bear comes home, and Mother Bear is stirring the soup, "Swosh, Swosh, Swosh."

Claire Bear is singing, "La, La, La."

Billy Bear is playing the drums, "Boom, Boom, Boom."

Teddy Bear is crying, "Wah, Wah, Wah."

The cow is mooing, "Moo, Moo, Moo."

And the pig is oinking, "Oink, Oink, Oink."

"It's too noisy!" shouts Father Bear. Once again he climbs the hill. "I love my family, but it's too noisy!"

"Bring the chicken into the house," says wise Grandma Bear.

"The chicken?" asks Father Bear.

"Yes, the chicken," answers wise Grandma Bear.

The next day Father Bear comes home, and Mother Bear is stirring the soup, "Swosh, Swosh, Swosh."

Claire Bear is singing, "La, La, La."

Billy Bear is playing the drums, "Boom, Boom, Boom."

Teddy Bear is crying, "Wah, Wah, Wah."

The cow is mooing, "Moo, Moo, Moo."

The pig is oinking, "Oink, Oink, Oink."

And the chicken is clucking, "Cluck, Cluck, Cluck."

"It's too noisy!" Father Bear cries. He climbs the hill one more time. "I love my family, but they are too noisy. And you should see the mess the chicken is making! What can I do?"

The wise old woman tells him to put the cow back into the barn and the pig into the pen and the chicken into the coup.

The next day, Father Bear comes home and Mother Bear is stirring the soup, and it smells so good. Claire Bear is singing, and it sounds great with Billy Bear's drums. Teddy Bear is crying, so Father Bear picks him up and rocks him back to sleep. "I love my quiet family!" says Father Bear.

Books About Noise to Read Aloud

Arnold, Marsha. 2006. *Roar of a Snore*. Illustrated by Pierre Pratt. New York: Dial Books for Young Readers.

Bright, Paul. 2003. *Quiet!* Illustrated by Guy Parker-Rees. New York: Orchard Books.

Dodd, Emma. 2002. *Dog's Noisy Day: A Story to Read Aloud*. New York: Dutton's Children's Books.

Glass, Beth Raisner and Susan Lubner. 2005. *Noises at Night*. Illustrated by Bruce Whatley. New York: Harry N. Abrams.

Most, Bernard. 1999. *Z-Z-Zoink!* San Diego: Harcourt Brace.

Rosen, Michael. 2007. *Bear's Day Out*. Illustrated by Adrian Reynolds. New York: Bloomsbury Children's Books.

Ideas for Playful Activities

Make Some Noise

Make some noise with musical instruments. Take turns playing the instruments loudly and playing them softly.

Play the sounds game in which children copy noisy actions, such as clap hands twice and hit knees. Have the children copy your actions.

Sing a Song

Sing a noisy version of "If You're Happy and You Know It" on the CD *Toddler Favorites* (Music for Little People, 1998).

8

Claire Bear's Kite:
Learning to Tell the Truth

Children will understand Teddy Bear's dilemma when he rips his sister's kite. Teddy Bear is afraid to tell the truth and tries to hide the kite. In the end, he learns that telling the truth is always better.

Characters and Story Pieces Needed

Claire Bear   Tree

Teddy Bear   Kite

Directions for the Story

Start the story with Claire Bear and Teddy Bear on the board. You can fly the kite off the board when demonstrating how graceful it is. Take Claire Bear off the board when she goes to get a snack. Move the kite around when Teddy Bear is flying it. When the kite rips, turn the piece over to show a rip.

FIGURE 8.1. Claire Bear's Kite

The Story

CLAIRE BEAR'S KITE

Claire Bear bought a beautiful green kite. She unrolled the string and let the wind pick the kite up and up into the sky. It looked so beautiful as it gently floated in the sky.

Teddy Bear watched as it twirled and danced in the wind. It looked like so much fun. When Claire Bear left the kite on the ground so she could go get a snack, Teddy Bear picked it up. He unrolled the string and let the wind pick the kite up, up, and up into the sky.

Teddy Bear thought it was very easy to fly a kite, so he decided if he ran just a little he could do some tricks with the kite. He started to run, and he watched as the kite followed behind him. He pulled the string and the kite dipped down. He jumped and the kite jumped. All of a sudden, the wind stopped blowing, and down, down, down went the kite. He hadn't been looking where he was going, and he was too close to a tree.

"Oh no," said Teddy Bear. He ran to catch the kite but it was too late. The kite crashed into the tree and fell to the ground. He picked it up [*turn the kite around*] and saw a rip in the beautiful kite.

"Oh no," thought Teddy Bear, "I can't tell Claire Bear. She'll be so mad!" Maybe it would still fly. He held the string and waited for the wind to pick up the kite. Up, up, it started to fly, but then it turned upside down and dove back to the ground. Teddy Bear hid the kite behind his back just before Claire Bear came back.

"Where is my kite?" asked Claire Bear.

"It flew away," said Teddy Bear.

Claire Bear started to cry. "My kite is gone?"

Teddy Bear felt so bad. He wanted Claire Bear to have her kite back, so he said, "I'm sorry I said it flew away, but I ripped it." He showed her the kite. Claire Bear wiped her eyes and took her kite. "You should have told me you wanted to fly it; I would have shown you how." Teddy Bear said he was sorry and fixed the kite with tape [*turn kite back over*].

"Now we can fly the kite again!" shouted Claire Bear.

"But not by the tree!" added Teddy Bear.

Books About Kites to Read Aloud

Emmett, Jonathan. 2004. *Someone Bigger*. Illustrated by Adrian Reynolds. New York: Clarion Books.

Hutchins, Pat. 1993. *The Wind Blew*. New York: Aladdin.

Lin, Grace. 2002. *Kite Flying*. New York: Alfred A. Knopf.

Williams, Vera B. 1997. *Lucky Song*. New York: Greenwillow Books.

Ideas for Playful Activities

Act Out a Rhyme

Five green kites in a line. [*Hold up five fingers.*]
All were green; all were mine. [*Point to self.*]
The wind blew and blew all day. [*Move hands for wind.*]
One green kite flew away. [*Fly hand upwards.*]

[*Continue the rhyme, substituting with four, three, and two green kites. Then say the last verse.*]

One green kite in a line.
It was green; it was mine.
The wind blew and blew all day.
One green kite flew away.

Get Active

Fly scarves to music. Try "Let's Go Fly a Kite" from the CD *Musical Scarves and Activities* by Georgiana Stewart (Kimbo Educational, 2002).

9
Teddy Bear the Magician: Hard Work Pays Off

In this chapter Teddy Bear finds out that sometimes you have to work a little harder to get the results you want. He thinks it would be easier to use magic to make a birthday gift for his sister but finds there is no easy way out. A gift is always better when you make it yourself. Teddy Bear finds that it is a lot more fun too!

Characters and Story Pieces Needed

Teddy Bear   Canvas

Paint brush   Flower (daisy shape)

Magic wand   Grass (orange, blue, green)

Directions for the Story

This is a silly story to have fun with. Put Teddy Bear on the board with the canvas. Teddy Bear holds the magic wand in one hand and the paint brush in the other. The children will think it is silly when you place the flower upside down first and then sideways. They will also love when you put the different colored grasses on the board. It makes it a lot easier to have the pieces in order before you start the story.

FIGURE 9.1. Teddy Bear the Magician

The Story

TEDDY BEAR THE MAGICIAN

Claire Bear's birthday is tomorrow, and Teddy Bear wants to make her a beautiful picture. Teddy Bear found a paint brush and a magic wand to help him!

"I can make a perfect picture for Claire Bear's birthday!" said Teddy Bear. Teddy Bear decided to paint a picture of a flower. He looked at the paint brush. He looked at the magic wand. The magic wand would be faster, so he chose the magic wand. He waved it over his head. He waved it in the air.

Hocus Pocus, magic wand.
Use your magic to show I care.
Make a pretty picture for Claire Bear.

Teddy Bear looked at the picture. "Is that right? No, the flower is upside down!"

He tried again. He took the wand, he waved it over his head, and he waved it in the air.

> Hocus Pocus, magic wand.
> Use your magic to show I care.
> Make a pretty picture for Claire Bear.

Teddy Bear looked at the picture. "Is that right? No, the flower is sideways!" Teddy Bear thought for a minute and decided to use the paint brush. It was more work, but it looked much better. [*Stand the flower the correct way.*]

Now Teddy Bear wanted some grass.

> Hocus Pocus, magic wand.
> Use your magic to show I care.
> Make a pretty picture for Claire Bear.

Teddy Bear looked at the picture. "Is that right? No, the grass is not supposed to be orange!"

> Hocus Pocus, magic wand.
> Use your magic to show I care.
> Make a pretty picture for Claire Bear.

Teddy Bear looked at the picture. "Is that right? No, the grass is not supposed to be blue!" Teddy thought for a minute and decided to use the paint brush. It was fun to paint the grass the right color. Green! Teddy Bear forgot about the magic wand and painted the rest of the picture. He was very proud of it, and he did it all himself!

It was the perfect picture for Claire Bear's birthday!

Books About Magic to Read Aloud

Cate, Annette. 2007. *The Magic Rabbit*. Cambridge, MA: Candlewick Press.
DiPucchio, Kelly. 2005. *What's the Magic Word?* Illustrated by Marsha Winborn. New York: HarperCollins.
Galdone, Paul. 1976. *The Magic Porridge Pot*. New York: Seabury Press.
Norac, Carl. 2006. *My Mommy Is Magic*. New York: Clarion Books.
Walsh, Ellen Stoll. 1994. *Pip's Magic*. San Diego: Harcourt Brace.
Watson, Richard Jesse. 2005. *The Magic Rabbit*. New York: Blue Sky Press.

Ideas for Playful Activities

Get Active

Play a game in which you or the children take turns being a magician and turning everyone into different animals. They will say the magic words and pretend to turn into different animals: "Hocus Pocus, you are a frog, a duck, a bear..."

Perform Magic

Show the children a magic trick. They will love the magic tree trick. It never fails to amaze. All you need is six pieces of newspaper, a pair of scissors, and a piece of tape.

1. Rip the newspaper down the middle lengthwise. You will have 12 pieces of newspaper.
2. Start to roll up one of those pieces of newspaper like you would a poster. Don't roll too tight. Leave about four inches at the bottom; then take a second piece of newspaper and overlap on the top. Continue to roll the paper. Continue to roll with that second piece until you have four inches at the bottom of that piece. Take a third piece of paper and place on top so that it overlaps, and continue to roll. Keep adding pieces of paper this way until all 12 pieces of newspaper are rolled up together into one tube. Place tape on the edge to keep the tube together.
3. Hold the tube upright, and cut slits about two inches down with scissors to make four leaves. You should have four flaps.
4. Place your fingers inside the tube and gently pull upward. The paper tree should grow right before your eyes.

10

Teddy Bear Visits the Moon:
There's No Place Like Home

This chapter has the children flying through space, dodging shooting stars, and spiraling through black holes. Teddy Bear goes for an adventure in space and wants to live on the moon but finds out there is no place like home!

Characters and Story Pieces Needed

Teddy Bear

Rocket ship

Moon

Stars

Falling star

Comet

Moon rocks (5)

Half moon

Directions for the Story

Put Teddy Bear in the middle, with the moon in the upper right and the stars scattered around. Place the comet and shooting star on either side of Teddy Bear. When Teddy Bear rides in the rocket ship, make sure his face shows through the little window and take off the moon. Pick up the rocket, and move it around the board while holding on to it and Teddy Bear. Place the half moon with the moon rocks on the bottom of the board so that Teddy Bear can land on it. Have Teddy Bear get out and walk on the moon. When Teddy Bear goes back home, put the yellow moon back in the sky and take off the rocket ship.

FIGURE 10.1. Teddy Bear Visits the Moon 1

The Story

TEDDY BEAR VISITS THE MOON

Teddy Bear looks up and sees the night sky. There are all sorts of wondrous things in the sky. He looks up at the moon. Maybe he could live on the moon. He would build a house and live there forever. "But how will I get to the moon?" thought Teddy Bear.

> Can he take a train?
> No, no train tracks!
>
> Can he take a boat?
> No, no water!
>
> Can he take an airplane?
> No, too far away!

He needs something that flies really fast and goes straight up into the sky. He thought about it for a moment and then said, "I've got it! A rocket ship!" He gets into the rocket ship and puts on his seatbelt.

The countdown starts. . . . 10, 9, 8, 7, 6, 5, 4, 3, 2, 1, Blast Off!

Up, up, and away! Teddy Bear holds on with both hands as the rocket lifts into the air. He looks out the window as he goes higher and higher. He watches the stars go by. He steers to the right. He steers to the left. He holds on with all of his might. He steers around a shooting star. He steers around the comet flying past him. Oh, no! He steers right into a black hole! Swoosh! Hold on! It's a bumpy flight! Finally he is out, and he sees the moon. He lands the rocket ship with a thud. His rocket ship is broken, but that's okay—he is going to live here forever!

Teddy Bear gets out and explores the moon. There is no gravity, so he floats and jumps through space. He jumps along until he finds a moon rock. One, two, three, four, five moon rocks!

It is fun for a while, but there is no one else to play with on the moon. He misses his family and friends. He decides not to live there after all. Teddy Bear wants to go home. How will he get back? His rocket ship is broken! He looks at the stars around him. That gives him an idea. He closes his eyes. [*The children can close their eyes also.*] He thinks of home and . . .

FIGURE 10.2. Teddy Bear Visits the Moon 2

He wishes upon a falling star!
When he opens his eyes he is back home!
"Welcome home, Teddy Bear!"

Books About Space to Read Aloud

Barton, Byron. 1988. *I Want to Be an Astronaut*. New York: HarperCollins.

Henkes, Kevin. 2004. *Kitten's First Full Moon*. New York: Greenwillow Books.

Landry, Leo. 2007. *Space Boy*. Boston: Houghton Mifflin.

Puttock, Simon. 2006. *Earth to Stella*. Illustrated by Philip Hopman. New York: Clarion Books.

Shaw, Nancy. 2008. *Sheep Blast Off!* Illustrated by Margot Apple. Boston: Houghton Mifflin.

Yaccarino, Dan. 1997. *Zoom! Zoom! Zoom! I'm Off to the Moon!* New York: Scholastic Press.

Yang, James. 2006. *Joey and Jet in Space*. New York: Atheneum Books for Young Readers.

Ideas for Playful Activities

Sing a Song

Sing "Twinkle, Twinkle Little Star" on the CD *Sing Along with Bob*, Vol. 2, by Bob McGrath (Bob's Kids Music, 2000).

Go on an Adventure

Listen to and act out "An Adventure in Space" on the CD *On the Move* by Greg & Steve (Young Heart Music, 2000).

11

Teddy Bear's Thanksgiving:
Being Thankful

In this chapter we join Teddy Bear and his family on Thanksgiving. It's Teddy Bear's favorite holiday. This year, it's his turn to go first to tell everyone what he is thankful for, but he doesn't know what to say. He doesn't have new things like some members of his family. He has to think of something fast.

Characters and Story Pieces Needed

Father Bear	Teddy Bear	Spoon
Mother Bear	Grandma Bear	Watch
Billy Bear	Table	Ball
Claire Bear	Pot	

Directions for the Story

Place the table in the middle of the board. Put Grandma Bear in the upper right corner with the pot and spoon. Father Bear (wearing the watch) and Mother Bear are on the right next to the table. Claire Bear (with her ball) and Billy Bear are in front of the table. Put Teddy Bear next to Mother and Father Bear. Move Teddy Bear around to the various family members as the story indicates. Let Teddy Bear take the pot, wear the watch, and play ball during the appropriate parts of the story.

FIGURE 11.1. Teddy Bear's Thanksgiving

The Story

TEDDY BEAR'S THANKSGIVING

It was Teddy Bear's favorite holiday. There would be turkey, cranberry sauce, mashed potatoes, and green beans. He would have a chance to say two of his favorite words: "Thank You."

Do you know what holiday it is?

It is Thanksgiving!

At Thanksgiving dinner everyone will take turns saying what they are thankful for. Father Bear and Mother Bear told Teddy Bear that this year he would go first.

Teddy Bear thought about it and was very nervous. He watched Grandma Bear stir the green beans in her new pot. He didn't have a new pot like Grandma Bear to be thankful for. Grandma Bear asked Teddy Bear if he wanted to stir the green beans in the new pot. He stirred and stirred.

Teddy Bear thought about it when he helped his father set the table. He didn't have a new watch like his father to be thankful for. Father Bear let Teddy Bear wear his watch while he set the table.

Teddy Bear thought about it while he watched Claire Bear play ball. He didn't have a new ball like Claire Bear to be thankful for. Claire Bear saw Teddy Bear looking at her ball. She asked Teddy Bear to play with her.

Then it was time to sit down and eat. Everybody asked Teddy Bear, "What are you thankful for?"

He didn't know what to say. He looked around the table and saw his family and remembered how everyone shared with him and played with him. He finally knew what to say.

"I'm thankful for my family!"

Everyone thought that was the perfect answer, and they ate a yummy Thanksgiving dinner.

Books About Thanksgiving to Read Aloud

Anderson, Derek. 2005. *Over the River: A Turkey's Tale*. New York: Simon and Schuster Books for Young Readers.

Jackson, Alison. 1997. *I Know an Old Lady Who Swallowed a Pie*. Illustrated by Judith Schachner. New York: Dutton Children's Books.

Levine, Abby. 2000. *This Is the Turkey*. Illustrated by Paige Billin-Frye. Morton Grove, IL: Albert Whitman.

Markes, Julie. 2004. *Thanks for Thanksgiving*. Illustrated by Doris Barrette. New York: HarperCollins.

Roberts, Bethany. 2001. *Thanksgiving Mice!* Illustrated by Doug Cushman. New York: Clarion Books.

Ideas for Playful Activities

Be Thankful

Have the children take turns telling everybody what they are thankful for.

Sing a Song

Sing "Over the River and Through the Wood" from Pamela Conn Beall and Susan Hagen Nipp's CD *Wee Sing Children's Songs and Fingerplays* (Price Stern Sloan, 2002).

Feed a Puppet

You will need a puppet and plastic pretend food (found at many dollar stores). Hold the puppet and have the children feed the puppet. Have the children name what kind of food it is and if they would eat it at their Thanksgiving dinner.

Act Out a Rhyme

Children love this rhyme! You can find more Thanksgiving rhymes on the Web site www.dltk-kids.com.

> The Turkey is a funny bird.
> His head goes wobble, wobble. [*Wobble heads.*]
> All he says is just one word . . . gobble, gobble, gobble!
> —Author unknown

12

A New Pet for Teddy Bear:
Finding the Perfect Pet

Teddy Bear wants a new pet, but can he find the perfect one? The children will love the silliness of the story in this chapter. The fun will continue with a game of animal charades or a funny song or two.

Characters and Story Pieces Needed

Father Bear	Dinosaur	Worm
Mother Bear	Chicken	Dog
Teddy Bear		

Directions for the Story

Place Teddy Bear on the board. Place the other figures on the board when mentioned in the story. Pause before you place the different "pets" on the board so the children can guess what animal Teddy Bear found. The children will love to join in when Teddy Bear says, "I've just met the perfect pet." The story ends with Mother Bear, Father Bear, and Teddy Bear on the board with his new pet.

FIGURE 12.1. A New Pet for Teddy Bear

The Story

A NEW PET FOR TEDDY BEAR

Teddy Bear wanted a pet more than anything. He thought about it every day. He wanted a pet with long ears that is cuddly, furry, and soft. When his class went to the museum, he was still thinking of what kind of pet he wanted. He saw a big dinosaur [*put the dinosaur on the board*] and decided he wanted a dinosaur! They were big and fierce. The perfect pet!

"I've just met the perfect pet!" cried Teddy Bear.

Teddy Bear thought about it for a minute. He wanted a pet that has long ears that is cuddly, furry, and soft.

"Does a dinosaur have long ears?" [*Give enough time for the children to answer.*] "No!"

Besides, the dinosaur was too big. He wouldn't fit through the door!

Teddy Bear was still thinking about getting a pet the next day when he went to visit a farm. Teddy Bear saw a chicken. Teddy Bear was very excited. The perfect pet!

"I've just met the perfect pet!" cried Teddy Bear.

Teddy Bear thought about it for a minute. He wanted a pet that has long ears that is cuddly, furry, and soft.

"Is a chicken cuddly?"

"No!"

Besides, a chicken would just lay eggs all over the house!

Teddy Bear was still thinking about getting a pet when he went for a walk. He saw a little pink worm. He was wiggling in the dirt. Teddy Bear wanted a pet more than anything.

"I've just met the perfect pet!" cried Teddy Bear.

Teddy Bear thought about it for a minute. He wanted a pet that has long ears and is cuddly, furry, and soft.

"Is a worm furry and soft?"

"No!"

Besides, the worm would just try to dig tunnels in the carpet.

Teddy Bear was sad that he couldn't find the perfect pet. He walked home where Mother Bear and Father Bear had a surprise for him.

It had long ears, brown fur, and was cuddly and soft. Do you know what his surprise was? [*Let the children guess.*]

It was a puppy dog!

Teddy Bear thought it was the most perfect pet!

Books About Pets to Read Aloud

Alsenas, Linas. 2007. *Peanut*. New York: Scholastic Press.

Campbell, Rod. 1982. *Dear Zoo*. London: Ingham Yates.

Cimarusti, Marie Torres. 2004. *Peek-A-Pet*. Illustrated by Stephanie Peterson. New York: Dutton's Children's Books.

Dodd, Emma. 2008. *What Pet to Get?* New York: Arthur A. Levine Books.

Keats, Ezra Jack. 1972. *Pet Show!* New York: Macmillan.

Ideas for Playful Activities

Play Animal Charades

Have the children take turns acting out different animals and letting the other children guess what animal they are. To help pre-readers choose which animal to be, show them cards you can print out from www.pbs.org/parents. Go to the "Parties" link and choose *It's a Big, Big World Party*. Look for animal charades and print out cards.

Sing a Song

Sing "Do Your Ears Hang Low?" on Bob McGrath's CD *Sing Along with Bob*, Vol. 2 (Bob's Kids Music, 2000).

Sing "My Dog Rags" on Bob McGrath's CD *If You're Happy and You Know It: Sing Along with Bob*, Vol. 1 (Bob's Kids Music, 2000).

13

Cooking with the Bear Family:

Working Together

Teddy Bear and his family are hungry for dinner. There is only one problem; they all want something different. What should they do? Only the smallest member of the Bear Family knows what to do. Only by working together can they make something that they can all agree on. The activities included will have the children making Rainbow Soup with scarves and singing about peanut butter!

The story in this chapter can also be used as a prop story. You would need a pot and the pretend plastic food (found at many dollar stores) mentioned in the story. The children can participate by adding the food.

Characters and Story Pieces Needed

Father Bear	Teddy Bear	Corn
Mother Bear	Pasta	Peas
Billy Bear	Carrot	Pot
Claire Bear	Potatoes	

Directions for the Story

Start with the Bear Family on the board. Add the food pieces when mentioned in the story. Have the children guess what kind of food the Bear Family is making together.

FIGURE 13.1. Cooking with the Bear Family

The Story

COOKING WITH THE BEAR FAMILY

It is dinner time for the Bear Family.
"What should we have for dinner?" asks Mother Bear.

> Mother Bear wants pasta.
> Father Bear wants carrots.
> Billy Bear wants potatoes.
> Claire Bear wants corn.
> Teddy Bear just says, "Peas please!"

What should they do? Everyone wants something different for dinner.

> Mother Bear gets the pasta.
> Father Bear gets the carrots.
> Billy Bear gets the potatoes.
> Claire Bear gets the corn.
> Teddy Bear just says, "Peas please!"

Mother Bear measures the pasta.
Father Bear cuts the carrots.
Billy Bear peels the potatoes.
Claire Bear mixes the corn.
Teddy Bear just says, "Peas please!"

Mother Bear says, "Wait, what is all this? This is too much food." But Teddy Bear knows what to do! Teddy Bear gets out the pot and adds water. Mother Bear puts in pasta. Father Bear puts in carrots. Billy Bear puts in potatoes. Claire Bear puts in corn, and Teddy Bear puts in the peas.

When it is done everybody sits down and eats yummy vegetable soup!

Books About Food to Read Aloud

Bonning, Tony. 2001. *Fox Tale Soup*. Illustrated by Sally Hobson. New York: Simon and Schuster Books for Young Readers.

Ehlert, Lois. 1987. *Growing Vegetable Soup*. San Diego, CA: Harcourt Brace Jovanovich.

London, Jonathan. 2001. *Crunch Munch*. Illustrated by Michael Rex. San Diego, CA: Silver Whistle/Harcourt.

Urbanovic, Jackie. 2008. *Duck Soup*. New York: HarperCollins.

Walter, Virginia. 1995. *Hi, Pizza Man*. Illustrated by Ponder Goembel. New York: Orchard Books.

Wood, Don and Audrey Wood. 1984. *The Little Mouse, the Red Ripe Strawberry, and the Big Hungry Bear*. Wiltshire, England: Child's Play.

Ideas for Playful Activities

Act Out a Rhyme with Scarves

This is a fun activity to do even with a large group. Hand out red, orange, blue, green, yellow, and purple scarves. You will also need a pot with a picture of a rainbow or a rainbow scarf hidden in the bottom.

Explain to the children that they are going to help make Rainbow Soup. When they hear the color of their scarf, have the children place their scarf in the pot. After everyone has had a chance to put their scarf in the pot, reach to the bottom and pull out the rainbow.

Let's make Rainbow Soup.
Add colors to the pot.
Yummy colors full of flavor. [*Rub tummy.*]
Stir it up and make it hot. [*Make stirring motions.*]

Red like apple, blue like berries, green like peas. [*Have children add these colored scarves.*]

Making Rainbow Soup is lots of fun!

Yellow like corn, purple like grapes, orange like oranges. [*Have children add these colored scarves.*]

Our Rainbow Soup is done! [*Pull out the rainbow.*]

Sing a Song

Sing "Peanut Butter" on the CD *Where Is Thumbkin?* (Kimbo Educational, 2000).

14

Teddy Bear Goes to School:
Where's the School Bus?

Teddy Bear can't wait for the first day of school. The story in this chapter will have children waking up Teddy Bear and helping him get ready for school. But where is the school bus? Children will learn all about different modes of transportation as they wait for the school bus. The activities in this section will have the children singing "Wheels on the Bus" and acting out *Brown Bear, Brown Bear, What Do You See?* (Martin, 1996) with puppets. They will also enjoy filling up Teddy Bear's backpack with school supplies.

Characters and Story Pieces Needed

Teddy Bear	Lunchbox	Train
Bed	Apple	Boat
Shirt	Car	Ocean
Pants	Airplane	School bus
Backpack		

Directions for the Story

The story starts with Teddy Bear in bed. The children can wake him up and stretch with him. Have the children pretend to comb their hair, eat breakfast, brush their teeth, and get dressed. Add the rest of the pieces when mentioned in the story.

FIGURE 14.1. Teddy Bear Goes to School 1

The Story

TEDDY BEAR GOES TO SCHOOL

Teddy Bear is sleeping. We have to wake him up. It's time for school!
"Wake up, Teddy Bear!"

Teddy stretches and combs his hair. He eats breakfast with a yum, yum, yum. He brushes his teeth with a scrubba, scrubba, scrubba. He gets dressed.

What color shirt will he wear? Blue.

What color pants will he wear? Green.

He needs his backpack, a lunchbox, and an apple for his snack.

He waits at the bus stop. He waits and waits. He hears something. Is it the school bus? It has four wheels. It has an engine. It goes, "Vroom, Vroom." It has a horn, "Beep, Beep." What is it?

It's a . . . car! [*Drive the car past Teddy Bear.*]

Teddy Bear hears something else. It is in the sky. Is it the school bus? It goes fast.

It's a . . . airplane! [*Fly the airplane over Teddy Bear's head.*]

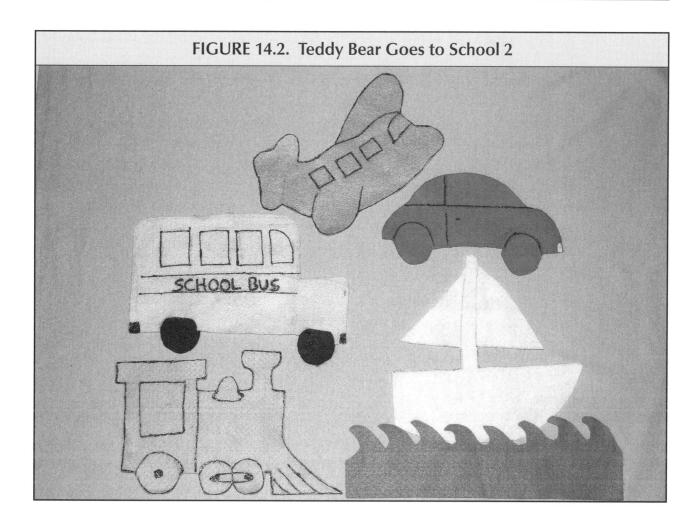

FIGURE 14.2. Teddy Bear Goes to School 2

Teddy Bear waits some more. Something is coming. Can you hear it? "Chugga chugga choo choo." What is it?

It's a ... train! [*Put the train on the board.*]

Teddy Bear hears something else. Is it the school bus? It has an engine, but wait—it's on the water. It's riding on the waves. [*Put the ocean on the board.*] What is it?

It's a ... boat! [*Put the boat on the board.*]

Teddy Bear still waits. Something is coming. It has an engine. It goes, "Vroom, Vroom." It's yellow. It has a horn, "Beep, Beep." What is it?

It's the school bus!

Bye-bye, Teddy Bear! Have a good day at school! [*The children will enjoy waving good-bye to Teddy Bear.*]

Books About School to Read Aloud

Crews, Donald. 1984. *School Bus*. New York: Greenwillow Books.
Henkes, Kevin. 2000. *Wemberly Worried*. New York: Greenwillow Books.

Hest, Amy. 1999. *Off to School, Baby Duck!* Illustrated by Jill Barton. Cambridge, MA: Candlewick Press.

Martin, Bill Jr. 1996. *Brown Bear, Brown Bear, What Do You See?* Illustrated by Eric Carle. New York: Henry Holt BYR.

Stoeke, Janet Morgan. 2007. *The Bus Stop.* New York: Dutton Children's Books.

Sturges, Philemon. 2004. *I Love School!* Illustrated by Shari Halpern. New York: HarperCollins.

Yolen, Jane. 2007. *How Do Dinosaurs Go to School?* Illustrated by Mark Teague. New York: Blue Sky Press.

Ideas for Playful Activities

Sing a Song

Sing "Wheels on the Bus" on the CD *Toddlers on Parade* (Kimbo Educational, 1985).

Fill a Backpack

Have children take turns putting school supplies in a backpack. You will need a backpack, crayons, glue, notebook, pencils, an apple, and a sticky name tag with Teddy Bear's name on it. Say the rhyme as the children bring up the school supplies and place them in the backpack.

> Help me fill Teddy Bear's bag.
> Can you find his name tag? [*Place the name tag on the backpack.*]
>
> He needs crayons in every hue.
> Red, orange, yellow, and blue. [*Put crayons in one at a time.*]
>
> Next on the list is some glue. [*Put glue in the bag.*]
> He'll need a notebook too! [*Put notebook in the bag.*]
>
> Five pencils and a snack.
> Let's put them in his backpack! [*Add five pencils and the apple.*]

Act Out a Story

An activity that a lot of children enjoy is acting out *Brown Bear, Brown Bear, What Do You See?* by Bill Martin Jr. (1996). Dltk's Web site (www.dltk-teach.com/books/brownbear/index.html) has some wonderful templates to print out to accompany the book. I print out the pictures (in color), laminate them, and tape them to popsicle sticks.

15

Teddy Bear's Picnic:
Fun for the Family

The Bear Family is going on a picnic. There's only one problem; they keep forgetting the most important thing: each other!

Characters and Story Pieces Needed

Father Bear	Teddy Bear	Cookies (2)
Mother Bear	Picnic blanket	Apple
Billy Bear	Glass of juice	Ball
Claire Bear	Corn	Tree

Directions for the Story

Put each family member in a different corner on the board when they are mentioned. Add the items that they have brought. The story ends with everyone together under the tree.

FIGURE 15.1. Teddy Bear's Picnic 1

The Story

TEDDY BEAR'S PICNIC

Mother Bear is going on a picnic.
She has found the perfect spot.
She brought a blanket and some juice.
But is there someone she forgot?

Father Bear is going on a picnic.
He has found the perfect spot.
He brought some corn on the cob.
But is there someone he forgot?

Billy Bear is going on a picnic.
He has found the perfect spot.
He brought some cookies
    and an apple.
But is there someone he forgot?

Claire Bear is going on a picnic.
She has found the perfect spot.
She brought her ball to play with.
But is there someone she forgot?

Teddy Bear is going on a picnic.
But where is everyone?
Without the whole family,
A picnic is no fun!

Teddy Bear finds everyone.
They picnic under a tree.
There's only one thing left
    to do . . .
They want to invite you and me!

FIGURE 15.2. Teddy Bear's Picnic 2

Books About Picnics to Read Aloud

Alborough, Jez. 1994. *It's the Bear*. Cambridge, MA: Candlewick Press.
Evans, Lezlie. 2007. *The Bunnies' Picnic*. Illustrated by Kay Chorao. New York: Hyperion Books for Children.
Goode, Diane. 2006. *The Most Perfect Spot*. New York: HarperCollins.
Hutchins, Pat. 2001. *We're Going on a Picnic*. New York: Greenwillow Books.
Jarrett, Clare. 2004. *The Best Picnic Ever*. Cambridge, MA: Candlewick Press.

Ideas for Playful Activities

Have a Teddy Bear's Picnic

Have a Teddy Bear's Picnic. Ask the children to bring in their favorite teddy bear or stuffed animal and pretend to go on a picnic. Spread out a blanket and ask what kind of food they would bring. Have a parade with the teddy bears and sing "Teddy Bear's Picnic" from the CD *Shake, Rattle & Rock* by Greg & Steve (Greg & Steve Productions, 2006).

Play a Memory Game

You can play this game with the story pieces from "Teddy Bear's Picnic." Place the blanket, corn, juice, cookies, apple, and ball on the board. Cover the board with a picnic blanket (small scarf) and lift one of the pieces off the board as you recite the poem that follows. Take the scarf away with the item hidden inside. Ask the children if they know what is missing while reciting this rhyme:

> Ants, ants, ants.
> They are hungry all day.
> But look out . . .
> They stole something away!

16

The Turnip:

Teddy Bear Can Do It!

Young children can relate to the theme in this chapter of building self-esteem and the attitude, "I can do it!" They understand what it means to try to keep up with older siblings or "bigger" children. They want to be just as big and strong as them. In "The Turnip," Teddy Bear wants to prove that he can help by pulling the turnip out of the ground. The books to read aloud suggested in this chapter are particularly wonderful in portraying the main characters as self-confident and triumphant. The activities in this section will show children how very special they are!

Characters and Story Pieces Needed

Father Bear	Teddy Bear
Mother Bear	Dirt
Billy Bear	Turnip
Claire Bear	Ribbon

Directions for the Story

This story is a lot of fun because the children really join in. Start with the turnip covered with the dirt, with only the green sticking out. Place Billy Bear next to the turnip. Have the rest of the Bear Family ready to join him on the board. The children can pretend to pull the turnip with the Bear Family. They love to call for the other characters to join Billy Bear. Put the blue ribbon on Teddy Bear as he helps pull the turnip out.

FIGURE 16.1. The Turnip 1

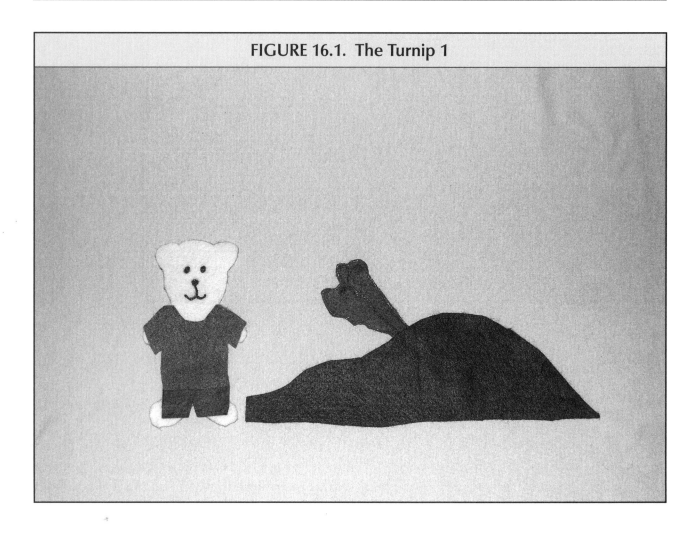

The Story

THE TURNIP

Billy Bear is growing a turnip. There is a contest at the fair tonight to see who grew the biggest turnip. The winner gets a blue ribbon!

Billy Bear is taking very good care of the turnip. He waters it and pulls out the weeds around it. Now it is time to pull it out of the ground.

He pulls and pulls
With all of his might.

He wants to win the ribbon
At the fair tonight.

The turnip doesn't budge. He needs help to pull the turnip out. He looks around for someone very strong. Who should he call? "Mother Bear, Mother Bear, I need your help!" he calls.

They pull and pull
With all of their might.

They want to win the ribbon
At the fair tonight.

FIGURE 16.2. The Turnip 2

Still the turnip doesn't budge. They need help. They look around for someone very strong. Who should they call? Father Bear! "Father Bear, Father Bear, we need your help!"

They pull and pull   They want to win the ribbon
With all of their might.   At the fair tonight.

Still the turnip doesn't budge. They need help. They look around for someone very strong. Who should they call? Big sister Claire Bear! Help them call sister bear. "Claire Bear, Claire Bear, we need your help!"

They pull and pull   They want to win the ribbon
With all of their might.   At the fair tonight.

Still the turnip doesn't budge. They need help. They look around for someone very strong. Who should they call? Teddy Bear? But Teddy Bear is so small! Can he help them?

"Teddy Bear, Teddy Bear, we don't think you can help," say the Bear Family. But Teddy Bear wants to help and says he'll try and try!

They pull and pull
With all of their might.
And with Teddy Bear's help
They win the ribbon that night.

Hooray for Teddy Bear! [*Children love to applaud for Teddy Bear.*]

Books About Building Self-Esteem to Read Aloud

Appelt, Kathi. 2003. *Incredible Me!* Illustrated by G. Brian Karas. New York: HarperCollins.

Carle, Eric. 1997. *From Head to Toe.* New York: HarperCollins.

Emmett, Jonathan. 2004. *Someone Bigger.* Illustrated by Adrian Reynolds. New York: Clarion Books.

Hutchins, Pat. 1971. *Titch.* New York: Macmillan.

Kraus, Ruth. 1945. *The Carrot Seed.* Illustrated by Crockett Johnson. New York: Harper and Row.

Piper, Walter. 2005. *The Little Engine That Could.* With new art by Loren Long. New York: Philomel.

Thompson, Lauren. 2008. *Wee Little Chick.* New York: Simon and Schuster Children's Publishing.

Ideas for Related Activities

Play Follow the Leader

Have the children take turns showing off what they can do. For example, one child can jump. Ask the group to follow what the child is doing. Take turns jumping, turning, wiggling, hopping, shaking, clapping hands, etc.

Perform the "I Am Special" Fingerplay

I tell the rhyme "I Am Special" as I search inside a bag (pretending to look for someone special) and find a mirror. At the words, "Someone very special" and "Yes, it's me," let the children look in the mirror as you hold it and move through the audience.

Where is someone very special? Where is someone very special?
If you search, you will see
Someone very special.
Someone very special.
Yes, it's me. Yes, it's me. [*Point to yourself.*]

17

The Snowman:
A Shape Puzzle

This chapter is all about snow and shapes. Children will never tire putting this snowy day puzzle together. What is more fun than learning about shapes while building a snowman? The activities included will have the children dancing like snowflakes and pretending they are snowmen!

Characters and Story Pieces Needed

Teddy Bear

Large, medium, and small circles for snowman

Two circles for eyes

Triangle for nose

Crescent for smile

Three squares for buttons

Square for hat

Rectangle for hat

Two rectangles for arms

Moon

Directions for the Story

Begin with Teddy Bear on the board. Place the pieces randomly on the board. Add the shapes when mentioned in the story, and have the children count with you. Take your time putting the snowman together the correct way. Most children will guess what you are making relatively quickly. Your audience will love it if you do the puzzle all wrong. For example, put the square on the bottom or use the crescent as the head, etc.

FIGURE 17.1. The Snowman 1

The Story

THE SNOWMAN

Teddy Bear loves snowy days. He walks outside, and this is what he sees . . .

Five circles, some big, some small.
> [*Put the circles on the board and count them.*]

Four blue squares, let's count them all. [*Count out four squares.*]
Three rectangles, two brown, one blue. [*Place the rectangles on the board.*]
Two crescents that stick with no glue! [*Place the crescents on the board.*]

One orange triangle, here it will sit.
> [*Place the triangle on the bottom of the board.*]

But where will all the pieces fit?
Let's move the pieces like so. [*Move the pieces around.*]
But wait, that's not how they go!

Will Teddy Bear know what to do?
I think he will, with help from you!

FIGURE 17.2. The Snowman 2

Let's help Teddy Bear, I know we can.
   [*Ask the children where the pieces should go.*]
Look, it's a . . . Snowman!

Books About Snow and Snowmen
to Read Aloud

Buehner, Caralyn. 2002. *Snowmen at Night*. Illustrated by Mark Buehner. New
   York: Phyllis Fogelman Books.
Ehlert, Lois. 1995. *Snowballs*. San Diego: Harcourt Brace.
Keats, Ezra Jack. 1962. *The Snowy Day*. New York: Viking Press.
Kirk, Daniel. 2004. *Snow Dude*. New York: Hyperion Books for Children.
LaReau, Kara. 2004. *Snowbaby Could Not Sleep*. Illustrated by Jim Ishikawa.
   New York: Little, Brown and Company.
Schertle, Alice. 2002. *All You Need for a Snowman*. Illustrated by Barbara
   Lavallee. San Diego: Harcourt.
Stojic, Manya. 2002. *Snow*. New York: Alfred A. Knopf.

Ideas for Playful Activities

Act Out Snowman Rhymes

The children will love acting out this rhyme with you:

A chubby little snowman [*Hold hands in front of you.*]
Had a carrot nose. [*Point to your nose.*]
Along came a bunny [*Hop like a bunny.*]
And what do you suppose? [*Shrug your shoulders.*]
That hungry little bunny [*Rub your tummy.*]
Looking for his lunch [*Hold a hand over your eyes.*]
Ate that snowman's carrot nose [*Pretend to eat.*]
Nibble, nibble, crunch!

For the next rhyme, I take five pictures of snowmen and tape them to popsicle sticks. Have five children stand in front of the room and act out the rhyme:

Five little snowmen in a row [*Hold up five fingers.*]
Each with a hat and a big red bow.
    [*Point to your head and make a bow shape under your neck with your hands.*]
Out came the sun, and it stayed all day
    [*Make a circle with your hands for the sun.*]
And one snowman melted away! [*Melt down to the floor.*]

[*Continue with four, three, then two snowmen, and then recite the last verse.*]

One little snowman in a row,
He had a hat and a big red bow.
Out came the sun, and it stayed all day.
And the last snowman melted away!

Dance Like a Snowflake

Play some classical music ("Snow Is Dancing" by Claude Debussy is a good choice), and let the children dance with snowflakes (scarves). They can turn, swirl, and dance and gently let their snowflake float down to the ground.

18

Billy Bear Visits a Farm:
Learning About Farms

Let's visit a farm! Billy Bear has a list of things to do, and he's not sure where to begin. Children will learn all about a farm and the animals that live on a farm. There are a number of great books and activities about farms. Have fun singing "Old MacDonald Had a Farm" with puppets or stuffed animals, and enjoy some farm riddles.

Characters and Story Pieces Needed

Billy Bear	Pig	Dirt
Bed	Chicken	Carrots (2)
Cow	Eggs (2)	Turnip
Milk bucket	Egg basket	

Directions for the Story

Place Billy Bear on the left side of the board and in his bed. Have the children wake him up with the sound of a rooster crowing. Place the bucket and the basket in each of Billy Bear's hands. Place the farm animals on the right side of the board when mentioned in the story. When you place the chicken on the board, hide the two eggs behind him. Place the vegetables with the green parts sticking out.

FIGURE 18.1. Billy Bear Visits a Farm

The Story

BILLY BEAR VISITS A FARM

Billy Bear woke up with the sound of a rooster crowing, "Cock a Doodle Doo!" He was farmer for the day and had a list of things to do. First on his list was to gather eggs. "Eggs?" thought Billy Bear.

"Where will I find eggs?" he wondered. Billy Bear walked outside and saw a cow, a pig, a chicken, and a garden.

Does a cow lay eggs?

No!

Does a pig lay eggs?

No!

Do you find eggs in a garden?

No!

Does a chicken lay eggs?

Yes!

How many eggs did Billy Bear find? He found two eggs and put them into his basket.

Next, he had to get milk.

"Where will I get milk?" wondered Billy Bear.

From a pig?

No!

From a chicken?

No!

From a garden?

No!

From a cow?

Yes!

He milked the cow, "Squirt, Squirt, Squirt!" He filled his bucket with milk.

The next thing on his list is carrots. Where will he find carrots?

Does a pig have carrots?

No!

Does a cow have carrots?

No!

Does a chicken have carrots?

No!

Does a garden have carrots?

Yes!

Billy Bear walks to the garden but can't find any carrots. Do you see any carrots? Then Billy Bear remembers that carrots are roots. They are underground! He digs up the green tops. [*Pull up the turnip first.*]

Is this a carrot?

No!

But there is more. He pulls and pulls and finally pulls up one, two carrots! His list is done. What a busy day on the farm!

Books About Farms to Read Aloud

Baddiel, Ivor and Sophie Jubb. 2007. *Cock-a-Doodle Quack! Quack!* Illustrated by Ailie Busby. New York: David Fickling Books.

Brown, Margaret Wise. 1989. *Big Red Barn*. Illustrated by Felicia Bond. New York: Harper and Row.

Cousins, Lucy. 2001. *Maisy's Morning on the Farm*. Cambridge, MA: Candlewick Press.

McDonnell, Flora. 1994. *I Love Animals*. Cambridge, MA: Candlewick Press.

Tafuri, Nancy. 2008. *Blue Goose*. New York: Simon and Schuster Books for Young Readers.

Zimmerman, Andrea. 1993. *The Cow Buzzed*. Illustrated by Paul Meisel. New York: HarperCollins.

Ideas for Playful Activities

Sing a Song

Sing "Old MacDonald Had a Farm." You can find the lyrics at www.dltk-teach.com/rhymes/macdonald/index.html. Use stuffed animals or puppets of farm animals, and have the children take turns making the sound of their animal.

Play a Game

Bring a bag with small toy farm animals in it. Read these riddles, and have the children guess what animal the riddle is about. Bring out the animal after they guess correctly.

Sometimes I am black and white.
I love to munch on grass.
I live in the barn.
I love to say one thing . . . Moo!

I love to run, run, and run.
I live in a stable.
Give me an apple
And I'll be a very happy . . . Horse!

I love to eat and eat
And roll in the mud all day.
Slop is a treat for me!
My favorite word is . . . Oink!

I love to eat seeds and corn.
I can sit on my egg all day.
I am a bird, but I cannot fly.
I'm a . . . Chicken!

19

Teddy Bear Is a Superhero:
You're Never Too Small to Be a Hero

Superheroes are a popular theme with young children. They love pretending to be superheroes while running, jumping, and flying. The story in this chapter shows that heroes come in all sizes. In the activities section, children will have fun acting out a superhero story and singing a song about superheroes!

Characters and Story Pieces Needed

Teddy Bear   Cape   Worm

Claire Bear   Mask   Dirt

Billy Bear

Directions for the Story

Start with Teddy Bear, Claire Bear, Billy Bear, and the worm on the board. Add the cape and mask when mentioned in the story. Have the children join in at the refrain. They can act out the movements. Place the dirt on the board at the appropriate time, and put the worm under the dirt.

FIGURE 19.1. Teddy Bear Is a Superhero

The Story

TEDDY BEAR IS A SUPERHERO

Teddy Bear wants to be a superhero. One day he put on a cape and mask. "I'm a Superhero!"

> He ran fast.
> He jumped high.
> He climbed the wall.
> He pretended to fly!

Big brother Billy Bear said, "You're too small to be a superhero." But Teddy Bear wanted to be a superhero. . . .

> He ran fast.
> He jumped high.
> He climbed the wall.
> He pretended to fly!

Claire Bear said, "You're too small to be a superhero." But Teddy Bear wanted to be a superhero. . . .

He ran fast.
He jumped high.
He climbed the wall.
He pretended to fly!

Outside on the sidewalk the bears saw a little pink worm. He was drying out in the sun. He needed wet soil.

Billy Bear said, "Just leave him."

Claire Bear said, "I'm not picking up a worm!"

Teddy Bear didn't think twice. He picked up the worm and carried it to the dirt. The worm disappeared with a happy wiggle into the ground.

"Wow!" said Claire Bear and Billy Bear. "Looks like you're the perfect size for a Superhero!"

He ran fast.
He jumped high.
He climbed the wall.
He pretended to fly!

Teddy Bear was a Superhero!

Books About Superheroes to Read Aloud

Bridwell, Norman. 2000. *Clifford to the Rescue*. New York: Scholastic.

Eaton, Maxwell III. 2007. *Superheroes*. New York: Alfred A. Knopf.

Hayles, Marsha. 2001. *He Saves the Day*. Illustrated by Lynne Cravath. New York: Putnam.

Heide, Iris Van Der. 2007. *A Strange Day*. Illustrated by Marijke ten Cate. Honesdale, PA: Lemniscaat.

McLeob, Bob. 2006. *SuperHero ABC*. New York: HarperCollins.

Pelletier, Andrew Thomas. 2005. *Amazing Adventures of BathMan*. Illustrated by Peter Elwell. New York: Dutton Children's Books.

Schwartz, Viviane. 2008. *Timothy and the Strong Pajamas*. New York: Arthur A. Levine Books.

Weigelt, Udo. 2007. *Super Guinea Pig to the Rescue*. Illustrated by Nina Spranger. New York: Walker.

Ideas for Playful Activities

Sing a Song

Sing "Superhero" by Milkshake on the CD *PLAY!* (Milkshake Music, 2006).

Go on a Superhero Adventure

The phone rings five times. [*Make the sound of a ringing phone.*]
The voice says, "Meow!" [*Say, "Meow!"*]
A cat is in danger.
Put on your cape and mask. [*Pretend to put on a cape and mask.*]
Let's dress for adventure.
Jump up high. [*Jump.*]
Run really fast. [*Run.*]
Look in the sky. [*Look up.*]
I see the cat stuck in a tree.
We'll have to climb. [*Pretend to climb the tree.*]
Climb and climb, up we go!
Save the kitty cat!
Carry him down and let him go! [*Pretend to carry the cat down in your arms.*]

20
Teddy Bear's Hanukkah:
Latkes for Everyone!

I am always amazed when my mother-in-law makes latkes. She takes one potato and one egg and makes one delicious latke after another. This story is based on her recipe, and the recipe is included at the end.

Teddy Bear and his family are celebrating Hanukkah. They are going to visit Aunt Sadie, who makes the best latkes in town. What will they do when Aunt Sadie runs out of potatoes? Aunt Sadie has to find the perfect recipe. A recipe for potato latkes can be handed out at the end of storytime. Children will have fun reading and singing about Hanukkah.

Characters and Story Pieces Needed

Father Bear   Aunt Sadie   Potatoes (5)

Mother Bear   Uncle Sol   Table

Billy Bear   Book   Triplets (3)

Claire Bear   Eggs (5)   Latkes (10)

Teddy Bear

Directions for the Story

Start with Teddy Bear, Aunt Sadie, and the book of recipes on the board. Place the table in the middle of the board. The children can count out five eggs and five potatoes. Every time the wind blows take a potato and an egg away. The children can act out the verses with you. At the end have the children guess how many latkes Aunt Sadie made. Give each character a latke and count again.

FIGURE 20.1. Teddy Bear's Hanukkah

The Story

TEDDY BEAR'S HANUKKAH

The Bear Family is celebrating Hanukkah, and that means eating latkes! Teddy Bear helps Aunt Sadie in the kitchen. Teddy Bear helps her count out five eggs and five potatoes. Can you help them sing this song?

> Aunt Sadie is in the kitchen,
> With a book of recipes.
> Five eggs and five potatoes. [*Hold up five fingers for each.*]
> She's making latkes for the family!
>
> A gust of wind through an open window
>   [*Children can wave hands like the wind.*]
> Sends a potato rolling out the door. [*Roll hands.*]
> Another gust of wind [*Wave hands like the wind.*]
> And an egg drops to the floor!
>   [*Make a pretend egg with your fingers and bring it to floor.*]

Aunt Sadie is in the kitchen,
With a book of recipes.
Four eggs and four potatoes.
She's making latkes for the family!

A gust of wind through an open window
Sends a potato rolling out the door.
Another gust of wind
And an egg drops to the floor!

Aunt Sadie is in the kitchen,
With a book of recipes.
Three eggs and three potatoes.
She's making latkes for the family!

A gust of wind through an open window
Sends a potato rolling out the door.
Another gust of wind
And an egg drops to the floor!

Aunt Sadie is in the kitchen,
With a book of recipes.
Two eggs and two potatoes.
She's making latkes for the family!

A gust of wind through an open window
Sends a potato rolling out the door.
Another gust of wind
And an egg drops to the floor!

Aunt Sadie is in the kitchen,
With a book of recipes.
One egg and one potato.
She's making latkes for the family!

A gust of wind through an open window.
Catch the potato before it rolls out the door.
Another gust of wind.
Catch the egg before it hits the floor!

Aunt Sadie's in the kitchen,
With a book of recipes.
One egg and one potato.
How many latkes did she make for the family?

1, 2, 3, 4, 5, 6, 7, 8, 9, 10! Just in time, because I hear a knock-knock at the door. Who's there? It's the rest of Teddy Bear's family!

How many bears do you see? Father Bear, Mother Bear, Billy Bear, Claire Bear, Teddy Bear, Uncle Sol, the triplets, and don't forget—Aunt Sadie makes 10!

Books About Hanukkah to Read Aloud

Capucilli, Alyssa Satin. 2002. *Biscuit's Hanukkah*. Illustrated by Pat Schories. New York: HarperFestival.

Kroll, Steven. 2008. *The Hanukkah Mice*. Illustrated by Michelle Shapiro. New York: Marshall Cavendish.

Levine, Abby. 2003. *This Is the Dreidel*. Illustrated by Paige Billin-Frye. Morton Grove, IL: Albert Whitman.

Rauchwerger, Diane Levin. 2005. *Dinosaur at Hanukkah*. Illustrated by Jason Wolff. Minneapolis: Kar-Ben Publishers.

Roth, Susan L. 2004. *Hanukkah Oh Hanukkah!* New York: Dial Books for Young Readers.

Ideas for Playful Activities

Sing a Song

Sing "Dreydel" on Bob McGrath's CD *If You're Happy and You Know It: Sing Along with Bob*, Vol. 1 (Bob's Kids Music, 2000). Another good version is "My Dreydel" by Raffi on his CD *Singable Songs for the Very Young* (Rounder, 1996). Bring in a few dreidels to show the children. They can take turns spinning them.

Act Out a Rhyme

These fingerplays along with many more can be found on the Web site www.preschooleducation.com under the link "Themes" and then "Holidays."

Five little latkes were sizzling in a pan. [*Hold up five fingers.*]
One went Pop, and then it went Bam.
    [*Clap hands on "Pop" and then slap the floor on "Bam."*]

Four little latkes were sizzling in the pan.
One went Pop, and then it went Bam.

[*Continue with three and two, and then sing the final verse.*]

One little latke was sizzling in the pan.
It went Pop, and then it went Bam.
No more latkes sizzling in the pan!

Another version is the following:

Five little latkes were sizzling in the pan. [*Hold up five fingers.*]
One jumped out and said, "Catch me if you can!"
   [*Put one finger down, and use a finger on your other hand to run away.*]
And it jumped and it ran all around the kitchen floor. [*Run in place.*]
When I turned around, it ran right out the door!
   [*Run the finger behind your back.*]

[*Continue until none are left.*]

Hand Out a Recipe for Latkes

AUNT SADIE'S POTATO LATKES

One large peeled potato, diced	Pinch of pepper
One egg	2 Tbsp. matzo meal
$1/2$ Small onion, diced	Vegetable oil
$1/4$ Tsp. salt	Applesauce (optional)

In a blender, mix egg, diced potato, and diced onion at medium speed until there are no more big pieces left. Pour the mixture into a mixing bowl, and add salt and pepper and matzo meal. Mix with a spoon until well blended. If needed, add additional matzo meal until the batter has an oatmeal-like consistency. Pour oil into a pan until it is $1/8$ inch deep. Preheat oil on medium-high heat. Drop spoonfuls of batter into the pan. Flip when the edges are brown. Place on a paper towel to absorb the excess oil. Serve with applesauce if desired, and enjoy! Makes about 12 delicious latkes.

Appendix

Patterns for the Teddy Bear Stories

The patterns to create the characters and props for the Teddy Bear stories are provided here for tracing or photocopying, or they can be printed from the accompanying CD. The chapters where each piece is needed are identified, and colors of felt or paper to use are suggested. (Except when indicated in parentheses after the listing of dimensions, images should be reproduced at 100%.) Some patterns are used for more than one character, and variations in color and features will help children differentiate between them. Use a permanent black marker to add features to the Bear Family and their friends.

Part of the fun of these figures is that you can embellish them any way you want to make them your own. For example, for the Bear Family you can glue on google eyes and add clothes made from pieces of fabric or felt. Decorate with sequins, buttons, and fabric paint. See the individual pattern descriptions for more ideas.

Cardstock is a good choice when using paper. It comes in a variety of colors and will work in the printer. Add features with markers or paints. Consider laminating the pieces to make them less fragile and last longer. Add a piece of self-stick Velcro to the back of each one to use on a flannel board, or attach magnetic tape to the back of the paper pieces for a metal board. I prefer felt pieces for these Teddy Bear stories. Most of the pieces will stick to the flannel board easily, but in the stories where pieces overlap, a Velcro tab should be glued on to keep it firmly attached to the board. Pieces needing the Velcro are noted.

The Bear Family Patterns

Father Bear (Tan)/Uncle Sol (Brown)—Page 85

Chapters: 1, 2, 5, 6, 7, 11, 12, 13, 15, 16, 20

Dimensions: $6^3/4$" wide and $10^1/2$" high (copy at 116.5%)

Optional embellishments: Use scraps of fabric for clothes; add google eyes. Dress up the figures with buttons, use ribbon for suspenders, and make glasses from yarn.

Mother Bear (Tan)/Grandma Bear (Gray)/ Aunt Sadie (Gray)—Page 86

Chapters: 1, 2, 5, 6, 7, 11, 12, 13, 15, 16, 20

Dimensions: $4^1/2$" wide and $8^3/4$" high

Optional embellishments: Use scraps of fabric for clothes; add google eyes. Use yarn to make glasses for Grandma Bear.

Billy Bear (Yellow)/Claire Bear (Gold)—Page 87

Chapters: 1, 2, 5, 6, 7, 8 (Claire Bear only), 11, 13, 15, 16, 18 (Billy Bear only), 19, 20

Dimensions: $3^1/2$" wide and $6^1/4$" high

Optional embellishments: Use scraps of fabric for clothes; add google eyes. Put a ribbon in Claire Bear's hair.

Teddy Bear (Tan)—Page 88 (top, left)

Chapters: 1–17, 19, 20

Dimensions: $2^1/2$" wide and 5" high

Optional embellishments: Use scraps of fabric for clothes; add google eyes.

Triplets (Brown)—Page 88 (bottom, right)

Chapters: 20

Dimensions: $3^1/4$" wide and 5" high

Optional embellishments: Use ribbons, buttons, scraps of fabric, and so forth to add distinguishing features.

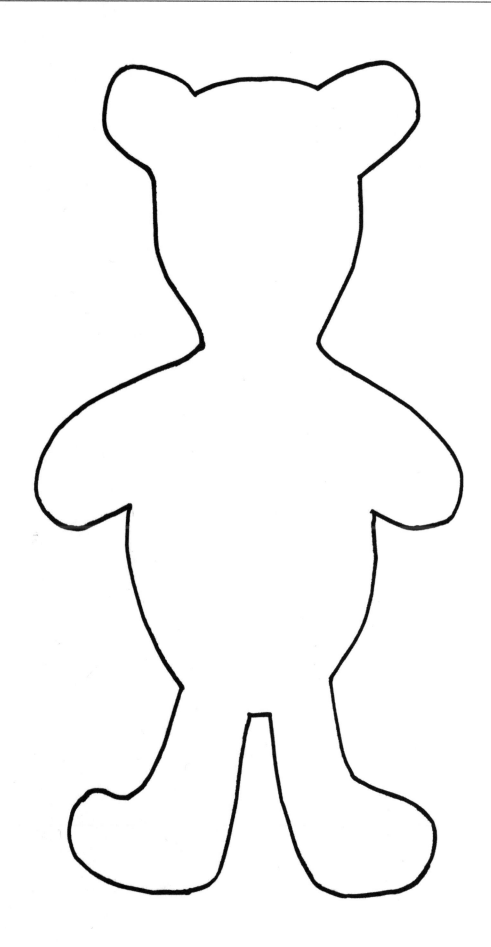

Animal Patterns

Chicken (White) — Page 91 (top, right)

Chapters: 1, 4, 7, 12, 18

Dimensions: $3^1/2$" wide and $3^3/4$" high

Optional embellishments: Add white feathers, a red felt wattle under the chin, and a red felt comb on top of the head.

Cow (White with Black Spots) — Page 91 (middle, left)

Chapters: 1, 4, 7, 18

Dimensions: 4" wide and $5^1/2$" high

Optional embellishments: Create a nose with pink fabric paint or pink felt to make it more three dimensional. For a cow bell, hang a small bell from a piece of ribbon or yarn, and tie it (or glue it) around the cow's neck.

Pig (Pink) — Page 91 (bottom, right)

Chapters: 1, 4, 7, 18

Dimensions: $4^1/4$" wide and $3^1/2$" high

Optional embellishments: Create a nose with pink fabric paint or pink felt to make it more three dimensional.

Bee (Yellow with Black) — Page 92 (top, left)

Chapters: 3

Note: Add Velcro to the bee.

Dimensions: $1^3/4$" and 2" high

Optional embellishments: Add the black with a marker or black fabric paint. Use netting for wings.

Butterfly (Blue) — Page 92 (top, middle)

Chapters: 3

Note: Add Velcro to the butterfly.

Dimensions: 2" and $2^1/2$" high

Optional embellishments: Add spots of color with felt or fabric. The antennae and body (not wings) can be covered with black fabric paint.

Ladybug (Black with Red Wings)—Page 92 (top, right)

Chapters: 3

Note: Add Velcro to the ladybug.

Dimensions: 1½" wide and 1¾" high

Optional embellishments: Use black felt, black fabric, or black fabric paint to add spots.

Worm (Pink)—Page 92 (middle, left)

Chapters: 3, 12, 19

Note: Add Velcro to the worm.

Dimensions: 2¾" wide and 1" high

Spider (Black)—Page 92 (middle, right)

Chapters: 3

Note: Add Velcro to the spider.

Dimensions: 1½" wide and 1½" high

Dog (Gray)—Page 92 (bottom)

Chapters: 12

Dimensions: 5½" wide and 4" high

Optional embellishments: Add a dog collar.

Dinosaur (Green)—Page 93

Chapters: 12

Dimensions: 5¼" wide and 7¼" high

Nature Patterns

Moon (Yellow) — Page 96 (top, left)

Chapters: 1, 10, 17

Dimensions: 2" wide and 3" high

Optional embellishments: Add a little yellow glitter to make it sparkle.

Clouds (White) — Page 96 (top, right)

Chapters: 1

Dimensions: 4" wide and 3³⁄₄" high

Flower (Tulip Shape) — Page 96 (bottom)

Chapters: 2, 3

Note: Make one yellow flower, one orange flower, and two green stems; add Velcro to the flowers.

Dimensions: 2¹⁄₄" wide and 2¹⁄₂" high (flower); 2" wide and 5" high (stem)

Optional embellishments: Make them more three dimensional by outlining the flowers in the same color fabric paints.

Flower (Daisy Shape) — Page 97 (top)

Chapters: 2, 3, 9

Note: Make the petals red, the center black, and the stem green; add Velcro to the flower.

Dimensions: 3" wide and 3" high (flower); 2¹⁄₄" wide and 4" high (stem)

Optional embellishments: Make it more three dimensional by outlining the petals in red fabric paint and the stems in green paint.

Dirt (Brown) — Page 97 (middle)

Chapters: 2, 3, 4, 16, 18, 19

Dimensions: 12" wide and 3¹⁄₂" high (copy at 177%)

Grass — Page 97 (bottom)

Chapters: 3, 9

Note: Make three strips—one orange, one blue, and one green—for Chapter 9.

Dimensions: 9¹⁄₂" wide and 1" high (copy at 140%)

Tree (Green Leaves and Brown Trunk)—Page 98

Chapters: 4, 8, 15

Note: Add the hole in the tree in light brown.

Dimensions: 8" wide and 11½" high (copy at 118%)

Sun (Yellow)—Page 99 (top, left)

Chapters: 6

Dimensions: 2¼" diameter

Ocean (Blue)—Page 99 (middle)

Chapters: 6, 14

Dimensions: 11½" wide and 3" high (copy at 169%)

Stars (Yellow)—Page 99 (top, right)

Chapters: 10

Note: Make four stars.

Dimensions: 1½" wide and 1½" high

Optional embellishments: For a twinkle effect, add a small amount of yellow glitter.

Falling Star (Yellow)—Page 99 (bottom, left)

Chapters: 10

Dimensions: 3½" wide and 2" high

Comet (Red)—Page 99 (bottom, right)

Chapters: 10

Dimensions: 3¾" wide and 2" high

Moon Rocks—*See* Cookies/Latkes/Moon Rocks (Pages 100, 102)

Half Moon—*See* Blanket/Half Moon (Pages 108, 110)

Food Patterns

Cookies/Latkes/Moon Rocks (Brown)—Page 102 (top)

Chapters: 10, 15, 20

Dimensions: 1"–1 1/2" diameter

Pot (Gray)—Page 102 (middle, left)

Chapters: 7, 11, 13

Dimensions: 4" wide and 2" high

Spoon (Gray)—Page 102 (middle, middle)

Chapters: 7, 11

Dimensions: 2 1/2" wide and 2 1/4" high

Pasta (Cream)—Page 102 (middle, right)

Chapters: 13

Dimensions: 2" wide and 1" high

Carrot (Orange with Green Leaves)—Page 102 (bottom, left)

Chapters: 13, 18

Dimensions: 1" wide and 3" high (carrot); 1" wide and 2" high (leaves)

Optional embellishments: Outline the carrot with fabric paint.

Potatoes (Brown)—Page 102 (bottom, right)

Chapters: 13, 20

Dimensions: 2 1/4" wide and 1 1/2" high

Corn (Yellow with Green Leaves)—Page 103 (top, left)

Chapters: 13, 15

Dimensions: 1 1/8" wide and 2 1/2" high (corn); 1 1/2" wide and 1 3/4" high (leaves)

Optional embellishments: Outline the corn and the leaves with markers or fabric paint.

Peas (Green)—Page 103 (top, right)

Chapters: 13

Dimensions: 3" wide and 1" high

Lunchbox (Blue)—Page 103 (middle, left)

Chapters: 14

Dimensions: 2" wide and 1³/4" high

Optional embellishments: Write out "Lunch" with fabric paint or glitter glue.

Apple (Red)—Page 103 (middle, right)

Chapters 14, 15

Dimensions: 2" wide and 2" high

Optional embellishments: Add a green leaf to the stem.

Picnic Blanket (Blue)—Page 103 (bottom, left)

Chapters: 15

Dimensions: 5" wide and 5" high

Glass of Juice (Purple)—Page 103 (bottom, right)

Chapters: 15

Dimensions: 1" wide and 1¹/2" high

Optional embellishments: Write "Juice" on the glass with fabric paint.

Turnip (Red with Green Leaves)—Page 104 (top, left)

Chapters: 16, 18

Dimensions: 1⁵/6" wide and 4" high (leaves); 2²/6" wide and 3" high (turnip)

Optional embellishments: Outline the turnip and leaves with markers or fabric paint.

Milk Bucket (Blue)—Page 104 (top, right)

Chapters: 18

Dimensions: 1¹/2" wide and 2¹/4" high

Eggs (White)—Page 104 (bottom)

Chapters: 18, 20

Dimensions: 1" wide and 1¹/4" high

Egg Basket (Red)—Page 104 (middle, right)

Chapters: 18

Dimensions: 3" wide and 2¹/2" high

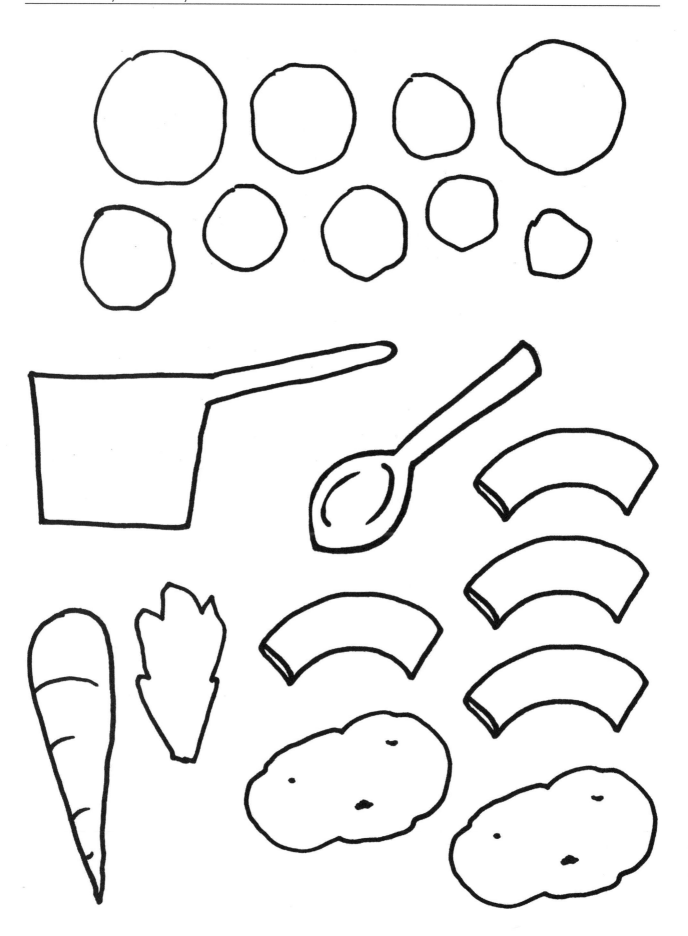

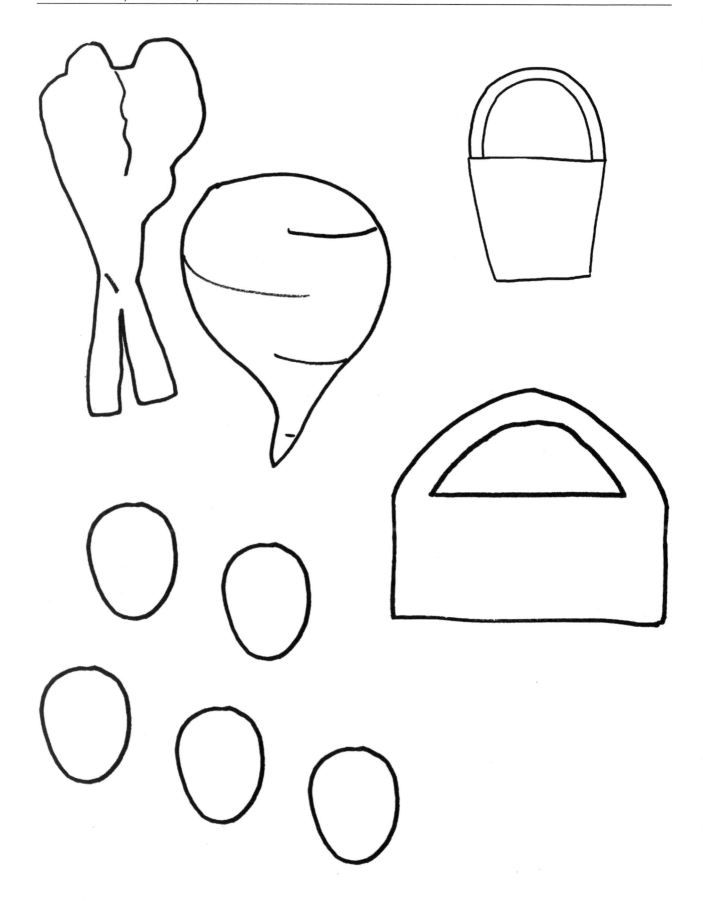

Clothing Patterns

Hat (Blue) — Page 107 (top, left)

Chapters: 3

Dimensions: 2½" wide and 1⅛" high

Optional embellishments: Outline the hat in fabric paint.

Watch (Brown) — Page 107 (top, middle)

Chapters: 11

Dimensions: ⅘" wide and 1½" high

Optional embellishments: Add numbers and dials with felt tip markers.

Shirt (Dark Blue) — Page 107 (top, right)

Chapters: 14

Dimensions: 2¼" wide and 2" high

Optional embellishments: Add a pocket made of felt or fabric.

Pants (Green) — Page 107 (middle, right)

Chapters: 14

Dimensions: 2" wide and 1¾" high

Backpack (Light Blue) — Page 107 (middle, middle)

Chapters: 14

Dimensions: 2⅙" wide and 2½" high

Optional embellishments: Add pieces of felt or fabric for pockets. Use ribbon or thick yarn for the straps.

Ribbon (Blue) — Page 107 (middle, left)

Chapters: 16

Dimensions: 1¼" wide and 2¼" high

Optional embellishments: Outline the ribbon with glitter glue or fabric paint.

Cape (Red) — Page 107 (bottom, left)

Chapters: 19

Dimensions: 3" wide and 2" high

Optional embellishments: Add the letter "B" for "Bear" to the cape.

Mask (Black)—Page 107 (bottom, right)

Chapters: 19

Dimensions: 1½" wide and ¾" high

Household Patterns

Mailbox (Gray) — Page 109 (top)

Chapters: 2

Dimensions: 3$\frac{3}{4}$" wide and 4$\frac{3}{4}$" high

Optional embellishments: Add a red flag with felt or fabric paint. Spell out "Bear Family" in any color fabric paint.

Couch (Dark Red) — Page 109 (bottom)

Chapters: 2

Dimensions: 9$\frac{1}{4}$" wide and 4$\frac{1}{8}$" high (copy at 140%)

Optional embellishments: Add pillows made of fabric scraps.

Table (White) — Page 110 (top)

Chapters: 2, 11, 20

Dimensions: 9" wide and 5" high (copy at 140%)

Bed (White) — Page 110 (middle)

Chapters: 2, 14, 18

Dimensions: 7$\frac{1}{4}$" wide and 4" high (copy at 140%)

Blanket (Brown)/Half Moon (White) — Page 110 (bottom)

Chapters: 2, 10

Dimensions: 6" wide and 1$\frac{1}{8}$" high

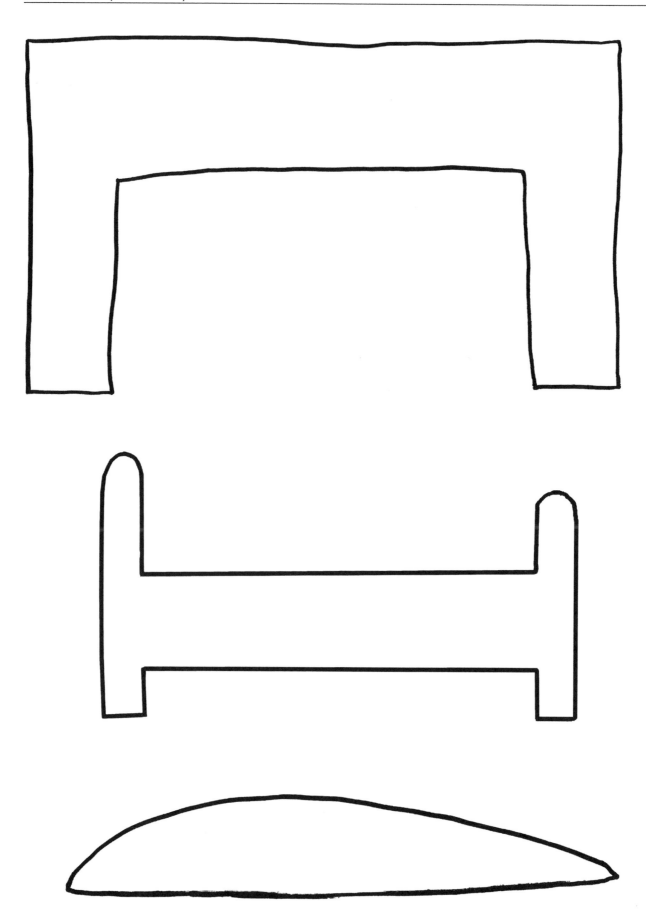

Vehicle Patterns

Car (Red) — Page 112 (top)

Chapters 2, 14

Dimensions: 8" wide and 4 3/8" high (copy at 122%)

Optional embellishments: Draw extras like tires and headlights with fabric paint.

Boat (White) — Page 112 (bottom)

Chapters: 6, 14

Dimensions: 8 1/4" wide and 6 1/2" high (copy at 122%)

Rocket Ship (White) — Page 113 (top)

Chapters: 10

Dimensions: 6" wide and 8" high (copy at 150%)

Optional embellishments: Add red felt flames to the bottom of the rocket. Add the letters "USA" in silver glitter.

Airplane (Gray) — Page 113 (bottom)

Chapters: 14

Dimensions: 8 1/2" wide and 4 7/8" high (copy at 150%)

Optional embellishments: Outline the windows and wings with fabric paint.

Train (Green) — Page 114 (top)

Chapters: 14

Dimensions: 9" wide and 5 3/4" high (copy at 150%)

Optional embellishments: Add windows, and color in the tires.

School Bus (Yellow with Black Tires) — Page 114 (bottom)

Chapters: 14

Dimensions: 9 1/4" wide and 7 1/8" high (copy at 150%)

Optional embellishments: Add windows, and write "School Bus" with a marker or fabric paint.

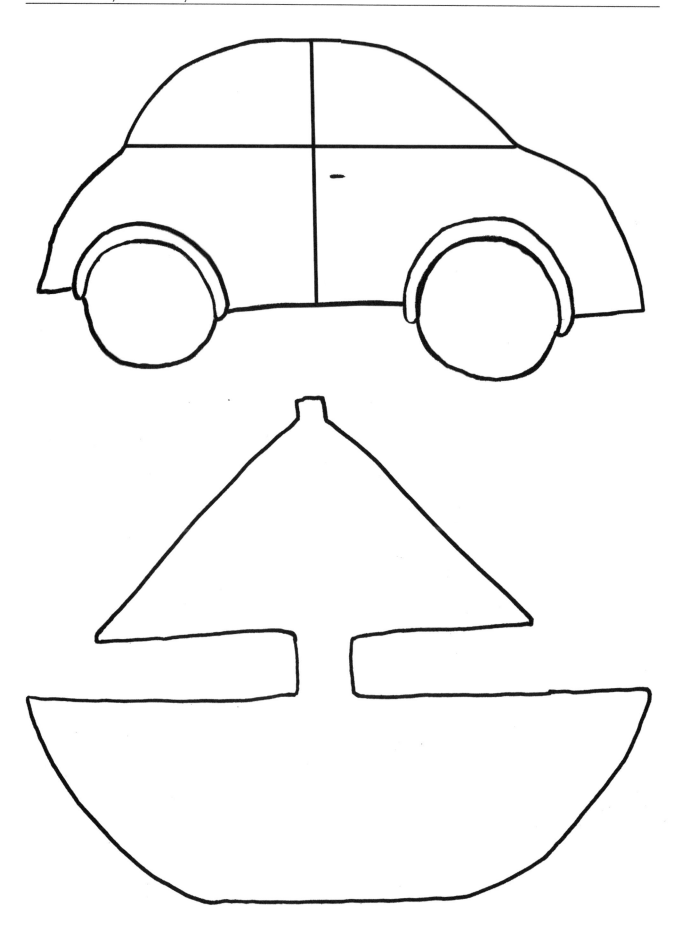

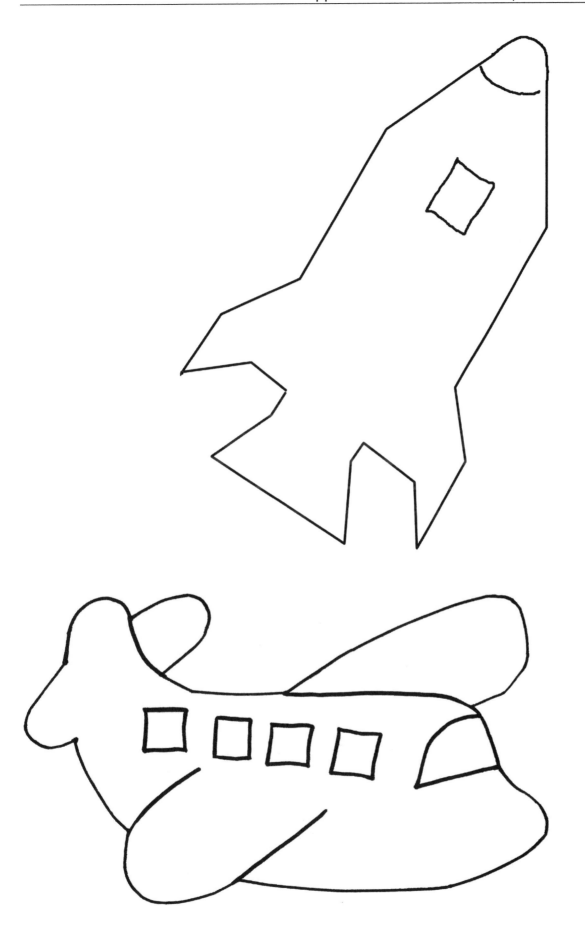

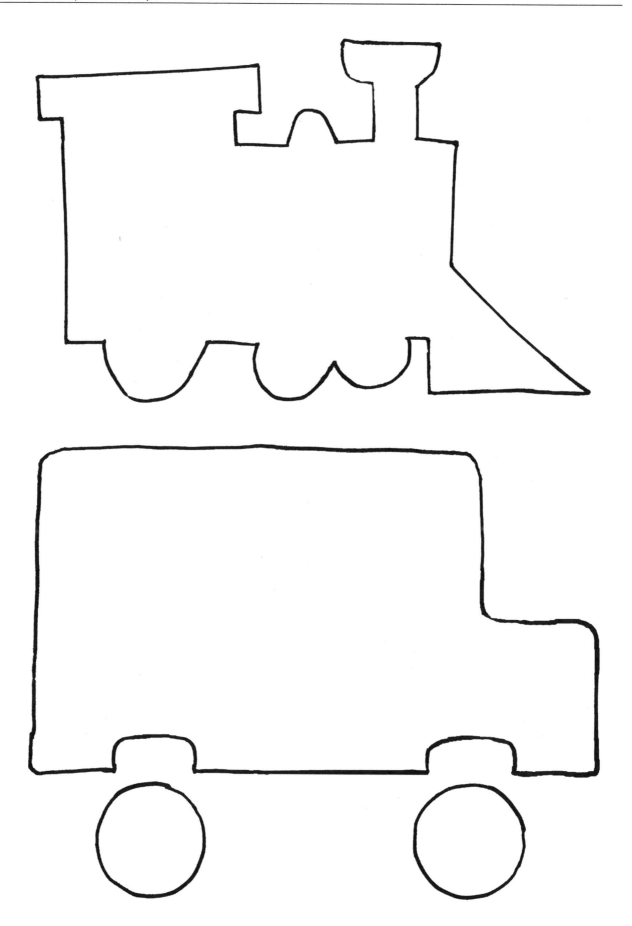

Playtime Patterns

Bat (Beige) — Page 117 (top, left)

Chapters: 1

Dimensions: 3" wide and 1" high

Optional embellishments: Fill in oval with dark brown fabric paint, and add gray tape around the handle.

Baseball (White) — Page 117 (top, right)

Chapters: 1, 15

Dimensions: 1" diameter

Optional embellishments: Add red stitching with fabric paint or a red marker.

Watering Can (Gray) — Page 117 (middle, middle)

Chapters: 3

Dimensions: 3" wide and 2" high

Shovel (Gray) — Page 117 (middle, left)

Chapters: 4, 6

Dimensions: 1" wide and 2½" high

Pirate Map (White) — Page 117 (middle, right)

Chapters: 4

Dimensions: 2" wide and 1¾" high

Optional embellishments: Color in features with markers, paints, or fabric paints.

Book (Blue) — Page 117 (bottom, left)

Chapters: 5, 6, 20

Dimensions: 3¼" wide and 2⅜" high

Optional embellishments: Outline the book with fabric paint.

Sand Castle (Brown) — Page 117 (bottom, right)

Chapters: 6

Dimensions: 3¼" wide and 3" high

Drum (Red with Blue Drum Sticks) — Page 118 (top)

Chapters: 7

Dimensions: 2½" wide and 1¾" high (drum); 1⁵⁄₆" wide and 1¹⁄₆" high (drum stick)

Optional embellishments: Outline the drum with fabric paint.

Kite (Green Kite with Pink Ribbon) — Page 118 (middle, right)

Chapters: 8

Dimensions: 4" wide and 4" high (kite and tail)

Optional embellishments: Glue three inches of ribbon of any color to the kite for the tail.

Paint Brush (Gray with White Brush) — Page 118 (middle, left)

Chapters: 9

Dimensions: 1½" wide and 2½" high

Magic Wand (Black and White) — Page 118 (bottom, right)

Chapters: 9

Note: Glue the shorter black strip onto the longer white strip.

Dimensions: ½" wide and 3½" high (white stripe); ½" wide and 2¾" high (black stripe)

Canvas (White) — Page 119 (top)

Chapters: 9

Note: Add Velcro to the canvas.

Dimensions: 9½" wide and 9½" high (copy at 150%)

Optional embellishments: Frame the canvas with wood strips, felt, or tinfoil to make it into a nice picture frame. Make sure the picture of the flower fits inside.

Ball (Orange) — Page 119 (bottom)

Chapters: 11, 15

Dimensions: 2" diameter

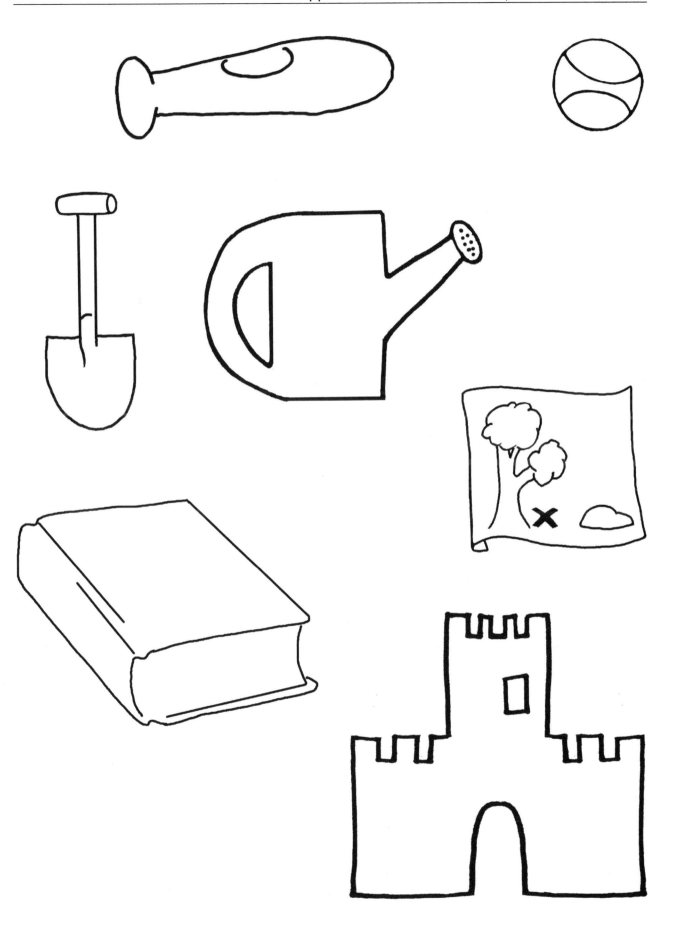

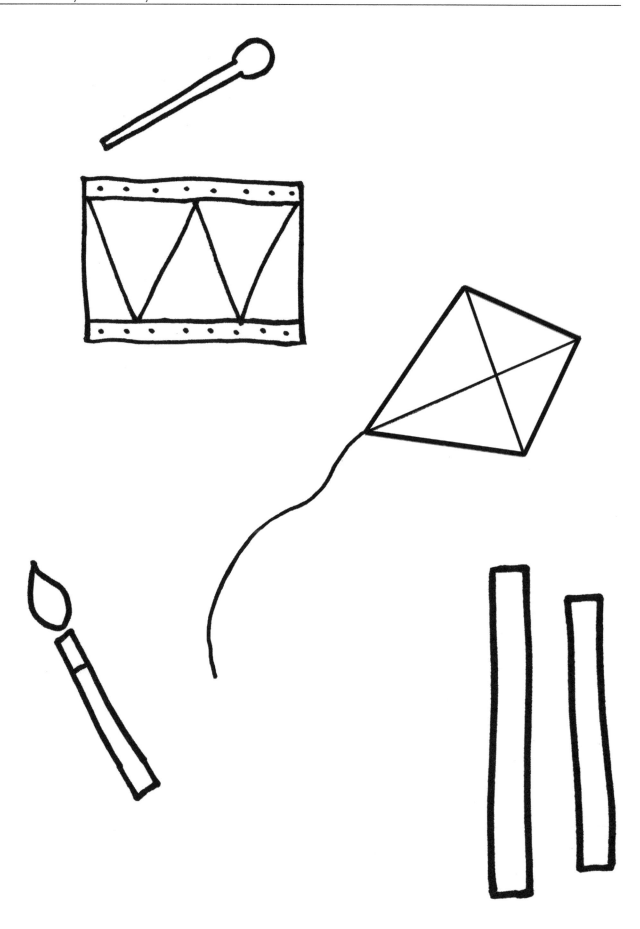

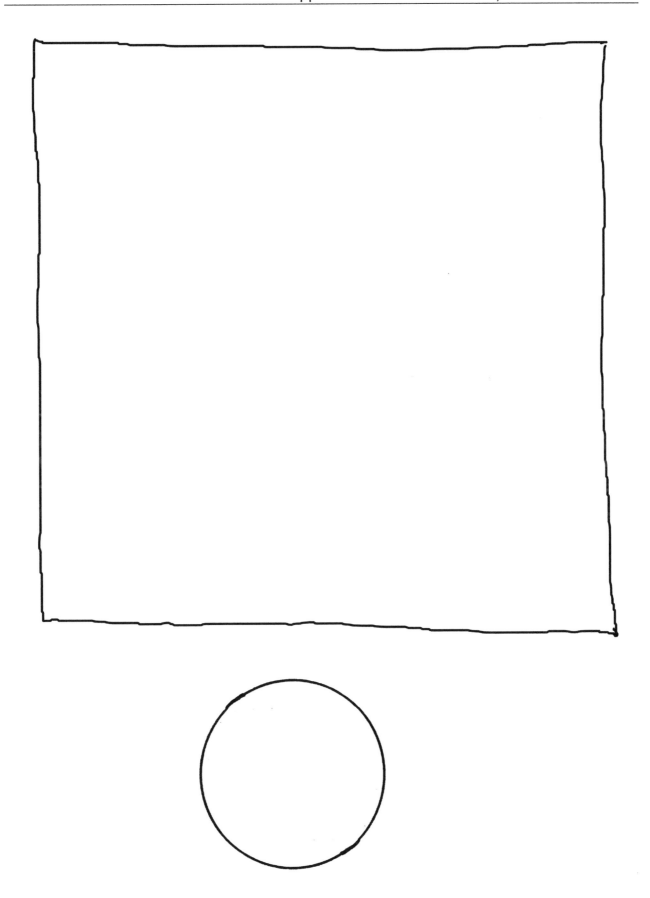

Snowman Patterns

Large Circle for Snowman (White)—Page 122

Chapters: 17

Dimensions: 5³/₄" diameter

Medium Circle for Snowman (White)—Page 123 (top)

Chapters: 17

Dimensions: 4³/₄" diameter

Small Circle for Snowman (White)—Page 123 (bottom, left)

Chapters: 17

Dimensions: 2³/₄" diameter

Two Circles for Eyes (Black)—Page 123 (middle, top)

Chapters: 17

Dimensions: ¹/₂" diameter

Triangle for Nose (Orange)—Page 123 (middle, middle)

Chapters: 17

Dimensions: ¹/₂" wide and 1" high

Crescent for Smile (Red)—Page 123 (middle, bottom)

Chapters: 17

Dimensions: 1¹/₄" wide and ¹/₅" high

Three Squares for Buttons (Blue)—Page 123 (bottom, right)

Chapters: 17

Dimensions: ³/₄" wide and ³/₄" high

Square for Hat (Blue)—Page 124 (top)

Chapters: 17

Dimensions: 3" wide and 3" high

Rectangle for Hat (Blue) — Page 124 (middle)

Chapters: 17

Dimensions: 4³/4" wide and 1" high

Two Rectangles for Arms (Brown) — Page 124 (bottom)

Chapters: 17

Dimensions: ¹/2" wide and 4" high

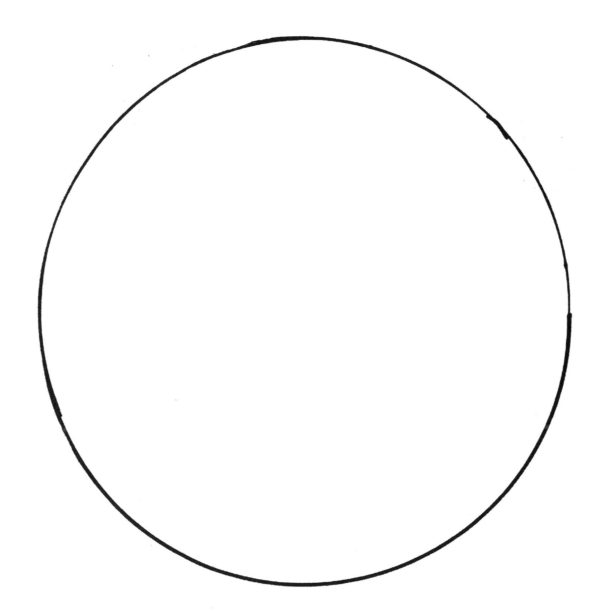

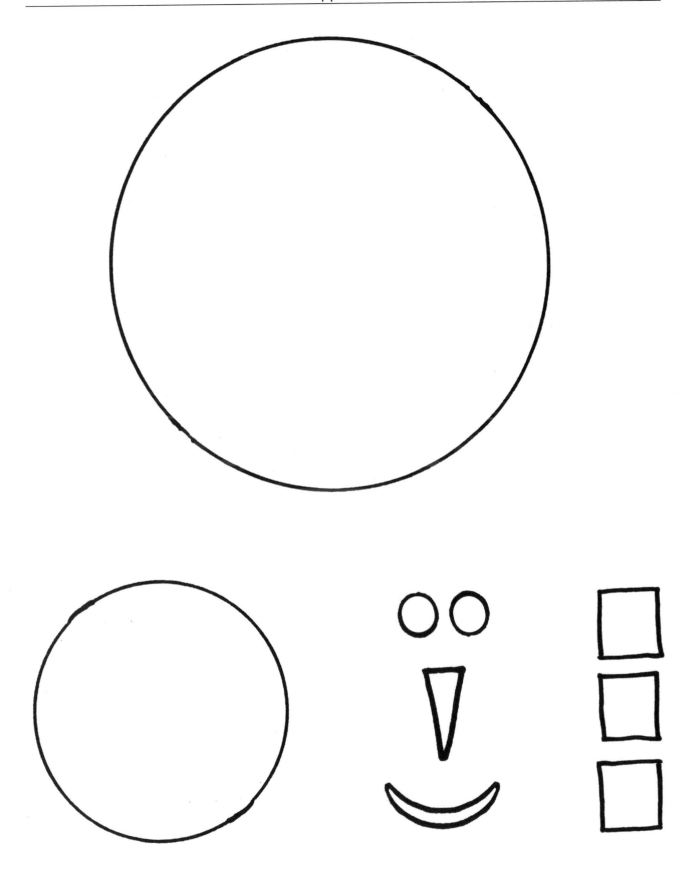

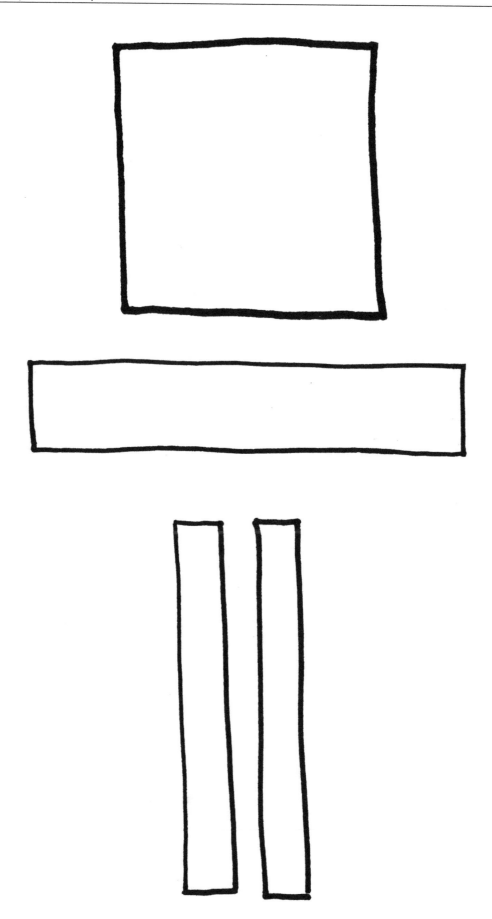

Theme Index

This theme index provides a quick-reference list of topics represented in the stories included in this book so that you can enhance your storytime programs using related themes.

Subject Index

About the Author

LaDonna Yousha has been a Children's Librarian and Storyteller for over ten years. LaDonna has worked at the Great Neck Library and in the busiest Central Branch of the Queens Borough Public Library and many of the 62 branches. She has planned and conducted countless storytimes as well as presented workshops on storytelling and the use of the flannel board to colleagues. In addition, LaDonna has had a few short stories, anecdotes, and games published in several periodicals and newspapers, including *Highlights for Children*, *Parents Magazine*, and *Newsday*.